CIRCLE OF CONVICTION

CIRCLE OF CONVICTION

By

B. Scott Gallie, Sr.

ISBN: 1-58500-986-5

1stbooks – rev. 8/8/00

About the Book

Did you ever wonder what life is really like in prison? Or, how the legal system operates to put someone there? Do prison guards carry weapons? If not, why not? Are conditions really that bad in prison? Should we execute more people waiting on death row, or should the death penalty be eliminated all together? How does an inmate get out on parole in Pennsylvania? Is there any rehabilitation going on in prison? If so, why do many inmates continue to return to prison after leaving on parole? In most cases, do we really have a choice as to whether we end up in prison or not?

If you are not sure or are undecided on the answers to most or all of these and many other questions about prison and prisoners, you need to read this book. Hopefully it will satisfy your curiosity on the subject, and make you think twice about how people end up living there. For those who do live there or have in the past, hopefully it will serve as a reference point and an eye opener.

The facts, statistics, stories, and information in the book were carefully researched and written from inside Pennsylvania's largest maximum security prison.

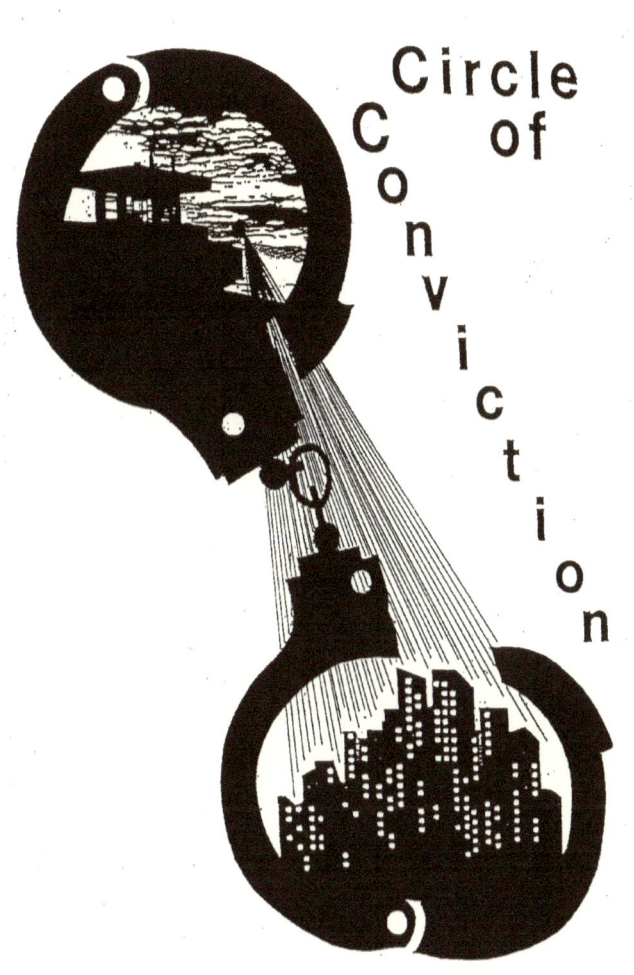

Circle of Conviction

Table of Contents

Introduction

Prison is a terrible place to live. Even though most inmates seem to adapt rather well, mostly due to necessity, it is still considered sub-optimal by the majority of the population at large. All of the rumors about prisons being like country clubs are simply not true, evidenced by the fact that no one is trying to drop their present membership at their own club and join up at the jail. In fact, if country clubs were anything like jail, they would have no members. The beds are hard, the mattresses are thin, the food is greasy, fatty and basically undesirable, and all of your neighbors and friends are convicted criminals. If you do not smoke, you usually end up buying cigarettes anyway, to use for trade and payment for something else you may want or need. You have no thermostat for climate control, only extremes of heat and frost. Hot and cold running water many times is just that - hot or cold, with nothing in between. It makes showers interesting at times-and quick. You are told where you can and cannot go - and when. You must be in by 9:00 p.m. and cannot come out again until 6:00 a.m. or shortly after, other than for work or a health emergency. To make sure you do not come out, you are locked in by the Correctional Officer, and remain there until you are once again released. Limited phone calls, limited visits, limited movement, limited lifestyle - prison is a terrible place to live. No one ever said it should be pleasant, easy, or comfortable, due to the purpose for which it was built. Nevertheless, the limits and restrictions appear to be endless. As the need arises, due to circumvention of the existing rules and procedures, change in rules or even completely new rules, can be implemented with a spoken word or the stroke of a pen. One person with the proper authority can shut down an entire jail - or likewise, have it opened up again to normal operation. In the name of justice, and as a condition of punishment, the State of Pennsylvania, as does other states, spends hundreds of millions of dollars yearly to incarcerate men and women convicted of crimes against society, ranging from petty theft to sex crimes and multiple homicides. The list of charges is endless, and so is the list of convicted people coming through the doors to serve time.

Once incarcerated, a new life begins. A new identity, a new look, a new way of survival. A metamorphosis if you will, that may birth an individual at times much less attractive than the previous specimen. Unlike the caterpillar's cocoon that shelters the ugly waiting to turn beautiful, the shelter of incarceration has the potential of taking the ugly and not so ugly, and creating a real monster. Whether it be the time, confinement, the loneliness, or the desperation and lack of hope, prison has a way of bringing out things in people that even they do not desire to see or deal with. An evolutionary phase of one's life that may not necessarily reflect in the genes, but may definitely affect their outlook and dreams. Some individuals tend to embrace the incarceration experience in a positive manner, making the proper preparation for a second chance at life in the free world. Others tend to absorb all of the negative attributes that jail has to offer, learning and practicing a way of life that may very well have an influence on their returning. What the end result will be after time served - if one's life is indeed enough time to complete it - always remains to be seen. After all, no human being is totally predictable.

Whether or not a person serves one day, one year, or a lifetime behind bars, there is absolutely no guarantee that he will never commit or take part in another crime. Crime is not predictable, just as the ones who commit it are not. When the factor of human nature is involved, anything is possible. One's personal "convictions" to proper morals, ethics, standards, and principles are the main determining factor as to who is doing what and why. A well-educated professional who feels little "conviction" about criminal activity, is just as guilty as the illiterate, underprivileged person who commits a crime out of ignorance, desire, or need. Or at least they should be. We all know how the legal system, along with politics and monetary persuasion, tends to find leniency with certain individuals at times. Race, social status, and prior record are no less contributing factors in our seemingly "justice inequity" system throughout the country.

This book for the most part, details the conditions of

"conviction" - prison life to put it simply - and the legal system that keeps it in motion.

The focus is on the Pennsylvania Department of Corrections and the justice system that is presently in use throughout the state. This collection of facts, statistics, personal views from convicts themselves, and many personal encounters with the system and its inhabitants, will hopefully provide very interesting reading and enlighten one to things never realized or known about convicts, their environment, and the entire penal system.

Employment at the State Correctional Institution at Graterford since 1981 has been no less than enlightening. Beginning with my first exposure ever to a jail, I had just left from my interview late one afternoon, just a couple of hours before I happened to turn on the television, and see dozens of State Troopers storming the front gate of Graterford in response to a hostage situation that had just occurred shortly after I left. Lasting almost one week before a peaceful surrender, this certainly made me think twice about working in a prison. Other events through the years, such as "Chicken Sunday" for example - in which a very volatile situation erupted over a tray of fried chicken, sending correctional officers to the hospital and running for their lives - revealed how dangerous and unstable the prison environment really is. Escapes, suicides, rapes, homicides, and countless altercations - some involving stabbings and beatings - are not uncommon in the prison environment. Graterford, being the largest prison in Pennsylvania, ranking fifth or sixth largest in the country, and housing some of the states most dangerous convicts, has for many years been the center of bad press for staff and convict alike. Though never experiencing a major riot in its entire history, despite its size and type of convicts that it houses, problems involving illegal drugs and contraband throughout the jail have plagued the institution for years. Staff involved in drug trafficking and other illegal activities has helped to fuel the ongoing fire of corruption and bad press.

In fact, an all out attempt was made to try and put a halt to much of this illegal activity and bad press in the fall of 1995. On the evening of October 23rd of that year, approximately 600 armed State Troopers and C.E.R.T. team officers (Correctional Emergency Response Team), along with U.S. Customs Service officials staged what was considered to be the largest prison raid in United States history, in an attempt to eliminate drugs and weapons, and crack down on drug trafficking among staff and inmates. Over one million dollars later, along with a new administration down through and including the Major of the Guards, change began to be evident. Mistakes that were made during a raid of this magnitude are still being rectified and compensated for, but nevertheless, some good change has taken place. Much needed re-vamping of personnel, policy, and procedures began opening the door to long - anticipated and much needed change throughout the jail. Some seemingly for the better, and some still questionable on the part of staff and inmate, but at least a change has begun to occur. The trick, of course, is to have it continue, and not just let things drift back to the way they were. It certainly is not perfect, and never will be, but it is a change that was truly needed. Some contend that it was purely politically motivated - which could very well be true in part or full - but most feel that the time was right - politics or not.

As I mentioned before, employment at S.C.I. - Graterford and a working knowledge of the State bureaucracy has been no less than enlightening and certainly a study in human nature! I have written about many of these enlightening experiences throughout the book, and hope to stimulate some thought in the readers' minds concerning convicts, prison, punishment, and the system that keeps it going within the ever widening, ever encompassing, ever "convicting" circle of conviction.

The System

Welcome to the world of the incarcerated, the realm of the unknown - known but to the inmates and those involved in detaining them. The subject is jail, and all those who inhabit it and make it operate. The system designed and functioning in Pennsylvania as the procedure of punishment for all those who have been convicted of a crime or crimes, and sentenced to serve time within the State Corrections System. So titled Pennsylvania's Department of Corrections (D.O.C.)

The business of incarceration is a big one. A multifaceted, multidimensional, multibillion dollar one at that. The limits are endless, and so is the ability to err. Undoubtedly, the larger the operation, the greater the chance of things not operating smoothly and properly. The more rules and policies there are to follow, the greater the chance there is that they will not all be followed. Unfortunately, as in many things, bigger is not always better.

This is blatantly exhibited in the world of jail. A world where time seems to stand still or at best move very slowly - while the system that controls it races ahead with great fury. While the policies and paperwork of procedural punishment continue to stack up, each day introduces to the system new lives to be torn down. A rather pedigreed process of penal procedure that predestines a punishment for criminal activity, profits from bad behavior, and continues to succeed from its never ending list of failures. An anti-criminal business that makes it its business to deal closely with criminals.

The system. Ah yes, the system. A rare animal. A bureaucracy within a bureaucracy. With each new sunrise it seems at times that we are captivated by more bureaucratic bewilderment and less cohesive corporate structure. A system of checks and balances that itself needs to be constantly checked and balanced. It appears at times that if it were not for disorder, there would be no order at all. That the key to consistency is in-consistency, and no matter how hard it tries to right its wrongs, it apparently has difficulty at times distinguishing right from wrong. An organization that consistently offers resistance to itself by way of redundancy and disorganized operations. A constant bombarding of bureaucratic attitudes, egos, and procedural power plays. Nonetheless, it continues to run and function within the purpose for which it was designed - to detain people convicted of crimes and sentenced to serve time.

My personal experiences with the system have been quite enlightening and educational to say the least. From the day of my interview, just hours before a week long hostage situation began, and continuing right on up to the present, it has been a total learning experience. Things in some cases that are not taught in class or found printed in textbooks about the D.O.C. or human nature in general, but rather lived experiences in and around the true prison environment. The enormity of Graterford and the wide variety of inmates it houses, surely contributes to its long list of problems and bad press throughout the years. Some people who work in other jails with smaller populations and staff rosters have difficulty relating to the magnitude of things at SCI-Graterford.

There are jails that house an entire population of inmates equal in number to only one, two, or a few of the 21 different housing areas and cell blocks at Graterford. Some of the states most dangerous criminals are housed at SCI-Graterford. This includes between 50 and 60 of the state's death row inmates at the present time.

There are approximately 1,200 employees at SCI-Graterford, which houses 3,300 plus inmates. This lends to the ongoing problems that exist in the prison. There are problems at Graterford that can and do exist in any other jail - simply because inmates are inmates, jail is jail, and people are people, no matter where you are. The ability to deal with these problems effectively is a whole different issue.

Communication breakdown is an ongoing problem at Graterford. From the beginning of my employment in 1981 right through to the present, I have occasionally missed meetings, appointments, visitors on official business, and deliveries, due to this communication breakdown.

Countless memos circulate throughout the D.O.C. in an

2

effort to keep staff and inmates informed as to policy, procedure, and other assorted news. Despite the fact that this goes on, many times people seem to be "uninformed" of changes and new developments. A memo received a day late, or sometimes the morning of a scheduled event or activity, usually defeats the purpose of the memo in the first place.

Verbal communication seems to be even worse at times, due to the fact that many messages just never get passed on. Jokes and gossip of all kinds generally seem to penetrate all boundaries, as in most environments, but vital information many times never gets delivered. The word of mouth communication deficit is especially bad at shift changes, and at times makes life harder for the relieving party, or the first shift the following day. Inmates many times have knowledge of information before staff. Again, this most likely exists more in this institution at Graterford due to its size, but nevertheless does abound.

Running a close second to the lack of communication, and as prevalent, is the overall practice of inconsistency. They seem to go hand in hand. It is not uncommon to have a Corrections Officer following or instituting a certain procedure at any given post, and if the officer is relieved for lunch, or off work one day, the rules and procedures change with the relieving party. Or, during shift change, the people being relieved may have done things one way, and the next shift all of a sudden has different rules. The shift to follow eight hours later, then institutes yet a different set of rules. Having this occur two or three times within a 24 hour period is not exactly synonymous with consistency. Laziness, irresponsibility, and procedural ignorance all help to contribute to the constant state of confusion that leaves inmates and some staff wondering at times just who is running the show.

The system, overall, for many years has had the reputation of being a good pay, not-work-hard set up. This reputation is very common among the state highway workers, with the "one or two men working while the others lean on the shovels or brooms" image, and has seemed to carry over to all state workers in general. The old "oh, you work for the state" cliche tends to demean and detract from the good side of state employee positions. There are certainly many good positions - and employees filling them - within the D.O.C. and throughout the entire state system.

Unfortunately, the D.O.C. does tend to have difficulty recruiting all optimal people to meet its staffing demands, due to the unusual working environment that prison offers. The constant friction between staff and inmates, fueled by every conceivable emotion, prejudice and feeling that exists, lends way to a very volatile, dangerous environment. To compensate for this, standards and requirements have had to be adjusted to include a wider spectrum of people, which tends to invite some that are not well suited for corrections work. Also common to the D.O.C., as in other state systems, is the hiring of close relatives in the way of husbands, wives, children, brothers, sisters, cousins and so on. This nepotism tends to create an inner network among employees, and many times, if one of these parties is offended in someway, they all may be offended within the family unit. Promotions, demotions, and other administrative acts can be, and have been, influenced by these family associations within each jail and throughout the entire D.O.C.

As a rule, the system tends to promote from within. In many cases, whether it be to higher ranks or to other positions, these promotions may provide less than optional staffing, especially in leadership areas. I have, on occasion, questioned some of the promotions to higher ranks that I have seen occur, especially after getting to know some of these individuals. I later found out that I certainly was not the only one who questioned them, and have often heard the saying "hey, if you can pass the test, you get the job", in reference to some of these surprising promotions to the higher ranks.

Some people I've talked with have even remarked that the "Peter Principle" is somehow incorporated into policy and procedure. For those unfamiliar with that, it basically states that one rises to his level of incompetence. Often observed in the jail at Graterford, is the practice of taking a person who is least qualified for a certain position within his specialty and placing him there. In this jail, as in any, I'm sure, there are areas where common sense and good public relations are a must to guarantee smooth operations. Ironically, these positions are staffed at times with people bearing these qualities in the minus numbers. By the same token, I've seen people removed from an area where they have been working and functioning well, and placed in an area that they knew nothing about. This practice can cause innumerable problems during the course of a day when it involves a high traffic area of the institution.

There are enough areas of everyday operating procedures to create mistakes without helping to create more. Many positions are often understaffed. This is due to absenteeism and staff shortage. As for staff shortage, budget is the buzz word. "It's not in the budget" is the common phrase. One statement often heard when dealing with staffing positions properly, is that "the State is poor; it can't afford that." The way some feel it really should read is "if the State is poor, it is not in money, just in planning." In all honesty, I cannot speak for every institution in the system as to the shortcomings and the problems that exist in each, but based solely on the feedback I've received through the years from inmates and staff associated with other jails, the general bureaucratic boondoggles that plague Graterford seem to exist throughout the entire network.

The system does have its advantages. It appears to be a set-up where one can enter at an early age, not work real hard, and make a career that will prepare him for a decent retirement. Pension, benefits, vacation, sick days - all the goodies people look for in a job, are right here. In many cases, without much responsibility. Sure there are positions within each jail that require diligence, intelligence, hard work, and a certain amount of dedication, but these appear to be the exception, not the rule. Statistically speaking, the system is very fortunate if even half of all the people it hires and trains remain employed for any length of time, especially within the ranks of Correctional Officers (C.O.'s). Many people find out after getting into the jail and its unusual environment, that it's just not for them.

I have met and gotten to know people in the system - mostly men - who would definitely choose this as the last place on earth to come and work. Because of economics and desperation for a job, they ended up there. They would tell you that they are not happy here and not really cut out for the environment, but simply needed an income and benefits. Others, of course, thoroughly enjoy it, or at least, tolerate it fairly well. Nevertheless, many have fallen into the revolving door situation of the system where needs are being met, but the system isn't necessarily meeting their needs. Unfortunately, some of these people have become underachievers in the dead end positions they have filled. This seems to be quite common within the ranks of correctional officers, but certainly not exclusively so.

It's interesting to talk from time to time with correctional officers and other D.O.C. people who are at the retirement end of the scale. After about 25 years or more with the system, they can usually make pretty fair and sometimes undesirable evaluations on the ever evolving corrections system. I thoroughly enjoy hearing stories from these seasoned individuals of the system, including those that date back to the life and times of the old Eastern State penitentiary at 21st and Fairmount Avenue in Philadelphia. They often make note in these stories of how "guards were guards and inmates were inmates", and how "everyone knew their place."

Furthermore, they will tell you that there is most definitely a marked increase in lack of communication between inmates and staff. The respect level has dropped drastically between officers and inmates, almost to a point of no respect. They say the new generation of C.O.'s coming in act as crazy as the inmates. I've heard inmates attest to that! After all, some of them came from the same neighborhoods and street corners. The problem is, the "homies" cannot seem to separate the street from the jail - not that it is easy, but definitely a must to be respected as an authority figure. Many of these individuals do not understand this until it is time to enforce the rules. Then, when push comes to shove, the "homie" status rises above the C.O. or authority status, and they stand there with egg on their face so to say. All the respect, what little there was, goes right out the window. Sort of like co-habitating with the lions until they think you are one of them, then pulling out the chair and whip to discipline them and make them do tricks. The results can be deadly.

I can recall hearing of a situation a while back on a cell

block where inmates were playing their radio's excessively loud. Complaints began to arise from other inmates, and eventually a "white hat" (a correctional officer holding the position of lieutenant or higher) sent word to the block officer to have the inmates turn the radios down, or confiscate them. This is all well and good, but remember, a command is only as good as the people who must carry it out. The officers seemed to have trouble with that order due to the fact that they were as much or more into the tunes as the inmates. They obviously had forgotten for a moment what their job actually was, and being captivated by the rappers on the radio, they seemed hesitant to carry out the order. Of course, the majority of the inmates noticing this who did not care for the music, once again had fuel for the fire involving discussions on lack of leadership and responsibility among officers and staff. Scenarios similar to this situation exist daily at Graterford, and most probably at other prisons, and only tend to continually lessen the respect an inmate might or should have towards correctional employees.

Officers years ago knew every inmate in their section by name, number, and work status, if applicable. For the most part, they were respected individuals for their professionalism and wisdom in controlling volatile situations. Most took a genuine interest in their jobs, and inmates knew them as people that they could go to with a problem and get results. Granted, the population was less, but so was the staff. Unfortunately, this same working, caring relationship does not exist today. Correctional employees in some cases have lowered their standards to a level which is the same or slightly above that of some of the inmates. An interesting observation is that many inmates notice this even before the civilians. They will tell you that with each new group of employees, they see it more and more. The end result - new employees, lower standards, less respect. A cycle that continues to perpetuate itself fueled by the ills of society. I must say, in all fairness, that there are many good C.O.'s and employees within the system, and certainly they should not be judged along with those of a lower caliber. If those who do not wish to conform to the system and follow the rules are not corrected or weeded out, their influence and habits could create a less than desirable work environment.

Almost a revolving door policy, like the proven fact that a certain percentage of inmates will always return to prison. As long as there is life on this planet, there will always be men and women, after being given the opportunity of freedom, that will return once again to a life of incarceration. Some for a short time and out again, and some for a longer time or even the rest of their lives.

Make no mistake about it :prison is big business. One of the largest and fastest growing in our society today. At this very writing, new inmates are being processed into the facility. The first area of the facility that inmates enter is the Assessment Unit. (The assessment unit is the area through which all new arrivals - including parole violators, new offenders, and temporary housing inmates - enter before being transferred for housing to others parts of the jail. The initial intake paperwork and procedures are done in this area). The assessment process includes the issuing of prison numbers, pictures, I.D. cards, clothing change, etc.) Some first time offenders, some repeat offenders with a new prison sentence, pre-release program violators, and parole violators (P.V.'s). Many days, approximately one half of the days intake here is made of men who came to prison, wasted some good years of their lives, and returned to freedom - only to fall back into the revolving door of justice, or injustice as the case may be.

There are men I talk to every day who come back as parole violators, most receiving technical violations for things they feel are very unjust and unfair. The common plea is simple and consistent -'They shouldn't have brought me back for such a stupid little thing." (Of course this is said in a variety of ways with just as many adjectives.) Nevertheless, the thinking is the same. Some of the common violations are things like not reporting as required by the conditions of parole: curfew violations, moving or changing address without notification, getting married without notification, being somewhere or with someone against parole specifications, domestic abuse (in any or all forms), traffic violations, working outside of a specified area, the use of drugs or alcohol or both, or of course committing a new crime. If arrested and found guilty of a new offense, new sentencing would then take place. Hardly a day goes by that I do not hear at least one of these cited reasons for returning.

It should be remembered that there are many circumstances and reasons surrounding recidivism. This wide spectrum of reasons for returning can and does include every situation from being falsely accused, to video - recorded identification of a crime being committed. One's economic status and social history are the contributing factors to one returning to prison. Guilty or not is another issue. The fact is the return rate is increasing, and more and more people are returning to the confines of incarceration.

I well remember working with a radiologist once during an X-ray exam on an inmate who appeared to be very familiar with the prison surroundings. I simply asked the inmate what his number was, to which he replied, "Which one?" I only needed his current number, and obviously by his response, he had been in jail previously.

Out of curiosity, the doctor asked him if he had been in jail before. To the doctor's total suprise, the inmate casually replied, "Yea Doc, this is my fourth time."

The doctor looked at him with total amazement, and simply asked, "Haven't you had enough of this?" The inmate humbly replied, " Yea Doc, I had enough the first time." The exam was completed, and the inmate politely said goodbye and left.

The doctor looked at me again in total amazement, and wanted me to confirm what he had just heard. He couldn't believe it - three previous sentences, three previous numbers, three previous jail terms served - and now, another new one. He simply looked at me, shook his head, and said, "Slow learner."

It is obvious by now, though, that the system of corrections is really not correcting all that much. This is greatly reflected in the high number of released inmates that are returned to prison. When observing the shortcomings and bureaucratic blunders that occur daily within the ranks of staff alone, this is not difficult to comprehend. I heard an inmate say once, that "the main problem with the whole system is, not that they just don't know - but, the scary thing is, that they don't know that they don't know." Or as a former employee who happens to be a good friend of mine used to say "you know, the Bureau of Corrections is really a strange name for this organization considering what really goes on here. It should be named the Bureau of Mistakes instead. " Back in those days you worked for the Department of Justice, Bureau of Corrections. In 1984, the title was changed to the Department of Corrections (D.O.C.).

If you study the D.O.C. operations manual, or O.M's as they are labeled, concerning policy and procedure, they appear very orderly and complete. Usually for every question, there is an answer. There is a directive, a policy, or something in writing to cover the situation at hand. Even though every institution runs a little differently due to physical layout or population, the standards and codes set forth are the same. All of the institutions are expected to follow the policies the same way. That's where we begin to encounter problems. Should work, and does work, are two different things. Don't forget, where the human being is involved, you will always have error. It takes human beings to carry out policy and procedures. The way it is supposed to happen on paper is not always the way it happens. In some cases, it never happens that way. The rule book is only as good as the enforcer. We so often see that policy begins to contradict policy. Sort of like using an eraser that constantly puts marks on the paper - the errors and corrections are never fully rectified. It is a means to an end, but the middle constantly grows larger and larger.

The redundancy that occurs within the entire system is at times nothing short of absurd. For example, a C.O. escorted a patient up to the X-ray room from our R.H.U. (Restricted Housing Unit). After being in the X-ray room a few minutes, he stated that he would be out the following week for specialized training in R.H.U. procedures. Hearing this, something did not jive. This prompted me to ask, "How long have you been working in the R.H.U.?" to which he replied "About 10 months now." I then asked him if this was advanced training needed to work there. He replied "No, pretty much standard procedure." At this point, I realized that he had been working down there for

10 months, doing a good job, but now it's time for the D.O.C. to give him his "specialized training."

In corrections, especially in a high security area where unstable, agitated, aggressive people are housed, you can get your brains beaten in and cause other people to get hurt as well by the time you are ready to receive your "specialized training" on how to deal with these kinds of individuals. Sort of like being hired as a lion tamer, and after having a few big cats jump on your back and try to eat you, you receive your training on "how to tame a lion". When interviewed from your hospital bed after regaining consciousness, you are asked why you were in there trying to do that job without any training or instruction. You calmly and painfully reply, "They wanted to see if I could handle the position first". Not to label these men as animals in a cage, but in reality the scenario is the same. Some of these individuals are as unpredictable as the weather, and cannot be taken lightly. Some are very predictable, and cannot be taken lightly. There have been many officers surprised and hurt by forgetting who they were dealing with for a second, or just not knowing how to deal with them at all. Of course, some Department officials and policy makers would tend to say that this is a rare occurrence, and does not happen that often, especially if experienced officers are there watching over the situation. This is all well and good in theory, but if you are the one that is being attacked and injured in a given incident, even one time is too much, especially if you don't survive to tell about it.

Politically correct, maybe. Documentarily correct, definitely. Practically correct, far from it. The old cover your butt routine. It looks good on paper when credentials are checked. "Oh yes, they had the training, right here. It's documented." In the opinion of many, if the state really wanted to cover their "bureaucratic and departmental derrieres," to put it bluntly, they would not send someone into an area to work without the training to work there, with the presumption that they will just catch on and adapt. It is difficult enough on a day by day basis to survive in the prison environment, especially as a C.O., without placing people in unnecessary danger no matter how unintentional or occasional it may be. Also, one thing common to and throughout the D.O.C., and other State systems, is documentation. Paperwork is a good part of its life's blood. And, during the course of everyday operation, whether it really makes sense or not, copy machines are kept warm and waiting for that next big opportunity to reproduce a document, or memo, or anything. The problem with this is that sometimes it appears as if the paperwork precedes good common sense and logical reasoning.

Sort of like my situation here over the years. Initially, I worked here at SCIG as a contract employee for the better part of six years. During that time period, I freely entered many parts of the jail including the R.H.U. areas, to instruct on medical procedures to be done in the department. This became a necessity if the patients ever expected to receive the exams on time and be informed of the procedures to be done. The system's continuity that was supposed to occur for patient information was next to non-existent. That's when my supervisor decided that it was best if we go directly to the patients' cells and discuss the procedures personally. This was done for special procedures, not routine studies. Nevertheless, it prompted travel by me to all parts of the jail. I learned the routes and procedures very well. Then, nine years later-yes, nine years - I was told that I would have to go through orientation to learn all about "the system". (which also included a tour of the jail.) No, this was not a mistake or an April Fools' joke. They were serious. Nine years later I was going through new employee orientation to learn the physical layout of the jail and its functions. By then, I could tell all of the "real" new employees how this thing functions. I know - by now there is a big question mark hanging in your cranium as to why.

Bureaucratically why? Typically why? Procedurally why? Why not? Documentarily why? That's it. It was not documented that I ever participated in this four week long department standard of saying hello. Simply, there was nothing on paper. Fortunately, my past "time served" did count for something. I only had to attend the "short course" for one week, seven and one half hours a day. A costly week for my employer, due to the fact that I had to be replaced, but very informative nonetheless.

Comically informative in one respect. I learned how, by policy, things were designed and supposed to operate. Of course, knowing the real side of things, it provided a nice contrast. I did learn a few real things that I did not know before, and that made it all worthwhile.

Speaking of waste in the system, which usually involves time, money, and effort, here is one story that remains vivid in my mind, and concerns nothing other than a leaking toilet - speaking of waste in the system.

It was only a short time since I had started in the jail, and I knew very little about inmates and the important role they play in the actual function of the prison. Inmates work throughout the jail in many of the maintenance, industrial and food service areas, among others. The state could never afford to employ all the civilians needed to do what inmates do at the price they are paid to do it. The inmates are supervised by civilians, but the bulk of the labor is done by the inmates themselves in these areas. At a cost of less than 50 cents per hour, you can't go wrong, especially for the amount of labor you are getting for that price.

At this particular point in time, much of the plumbing at Graterford was old. The potential for it to fail or break in some way had evolved into a day to day probability. On this one particular day, the reality of commode plumbing failure had found its way to the bathroom in X-ray and prompt repair was definitely a priority. This is where bureaucracy versus practicability occurs.

Being a fairly new employee, I had to find out how to get it fixed, not knowing the procedures. My supervisor begins by telling me to call maintenance. So, I scan the phone list of the institution, and call maintenance. They tell me I must call the plumbing shop, after my describing the problem in detail of course.

Once again, I checked the phone list and called the plumbing shop number, only to be told that I must fill out a work order. I stressed to them that this water is running full tilt, but, paperwork must prevail.

Now, who has work orders, and where do I get one? After

that, whom do I give it to? All questions my supervisor hopefully could answer without delay. I quickly found out that my supervisor is now in a meeting somewhere, for an unknown amount of time. No one else seems to know where these so - called work orders are kept, or do not care at the moment to tell me, even if they do know. So, the water continued to run at many gallons per hour.

As hours go by, with gallons of water going into the sewer due to bureaucratic impedance to practicality, I happened to talk to an inmate who knows many of the inmate plumbers. By this time of the day, the chances of getting something fixed are getting less and less, while the water is running more and more. The inmate says "Hey, forget the paperwork, I'll call the block and get a plumber down here right now."

As far as I knew, this was just another fruitless effort, but I was willing to give him the benefit of the doubt. I said to this well meaning inmate, "Hey thanks, but I doubt if it will do any good." He made a phone call, and said "He'll be here to hook you up in a minute." I did not see him again the rest of the day. I assumed his verbiage meant that someone would be coming around to shut off the water.

So, here we are hours later, no supervisor, no work orders, no one who can get me a work order, and the plumbers do not care to see or hear from me until I get a work order. Whatever happened to emergency service?

Nevertheless, fifteen minutes later a knock disturbed the solemn sound of running water, unfortunately not by a peaceful river bank - and behold, an inmate plumber appears with tools in hand. The problem is fixed within five minutes. No paperwork, no bureaucratic boondoggles, and no thanks to the system at large.

I've had other situations occur in the past with the same scenario but different details. Unfortunately, or fortunately for me, knowing certain people and having established certain lines of communication among inmates and staff alike, what began as a molehill type problem remained as such, and did not escalate to become a mountain of a problem until being solved. Inmates tend to keep things short and to the point, especially to acquire

14

things they want or need. The system as it appears, is not really interested in speed and efficiency, but rather procedural conduct, regardless of the cost.

I saw this blatantly demonstrated with my pay check procedures, again, as a contract employee in the early 1980's. From the day I turned in my pay voucher with my hours worked, I was very fortunate if I saw a pay check four weeks later. I can recall waiting as long as seven weeks, and even an exceptionally fast arrival after three weeks, but usually four to six weeks was the average time span. Why so long? Simple. Procedural Bureaucratic boondoggles. As my pay voucher made its way from hand to hand and desk to desk, the possibilities for delay were limitless. People on vacation, people out sick, or people who just didn't feel like being productive on a certain day or days, all helped to contribute to the already redundant process in force, not to mention understaffing. Why it was necessary to have five or six signatures and a stamp including the State Treasurer to validate my measly little part - time check was a mystery to me. But of course, when you see all the people involved, then the delay in payment is no mystery either. The real mystery is that the system has continued to function all this time, and there are actually rumors in the wind that changes are occurring for the better to help expedite these processes. One can only hope and pray.

Many times, due to common and ongoing mistakes and mismanagement throughout the D.O.C., taxpayer dollars at times are not used to the best advantage. The bureaucracy is obviously able to juggle funds and defray costs incurred due to unexpected or unbudgeted occurrences, much unlike most private businesses. If showing a profit to stay solvent was the bottom line, the state system would have been out of business many years ago.

This was clearly demonstrated to me in the mid 1980's being personally involved with the purchase of new X-ray equipment for SCI-Graterford.

An operation that should have meant a two or three week delay in the X-ray services to inmates, turned into a nine month taxpayer-burdened nightmare. A very costly nightmare at the

15

least, with inmates being escorted out to the hospital daily for routine studies that could have been performed for a fraction of the cost at the institution. Added on to the medical costs incurred were extra salary costs for officers to escort the inmates, extra wear and tear to state vehicles, and the extra security risk factor in moving all of the inmates during that period of time.

As for myself, I was a part-time employee then, and the delay cost me sixteen to twenty hours per week in salary over the nine months that I was not working.

It all began with a vital piece of equipment that was required to power the new X-ray unit. That equipment was never ordered by the institution as it should have been in the first place. Then when it was ordered, it was not done correctly, and was not adequate. By then, the old X-ray machine had been removed and the new one was in place and assembled. All that was needed was the adequate power to operate it. When the proper equipment was finally ordered, it then took months to have it fabricated and shipped. Meanwhile, the new X-ray unit sat idle just waiting for the power to run it.

Finally, after the delivery and installation of the new power equipment, it was time to power up the new machine and calibrate it. Upon attempting this, the machine would not turn on. Prior to this many months' delay, it would at least turn on for a few seconds.

Following three days of diagnostic evaluation performed by two installation technicians working eight hours per day, it was discovered that some wires had been mysteriously switched within the X-ray generator during the many months of idle waiting.

Finally, the damage was repaired, the unit was calibrated, I was called back to work, and the SCI-Graterford X-ray deparment was back in operation - nine very costly months after the original shut down.

Being the largest and most costly bureaucratic blunder that I have ever personally heard of or been involved with since the day I began employment at SCI-G, it could have all been easily avoided. A clear case of miscommunication, mismanagement, irresponsibility, lack of concern, lack of accountability, and a general attitude of "who gives a rip" certainly proved to be highly counter - productive and cost - ineffective.

Even worse, I was told at a later date after being back in service, that it was "just one of those things - it wasn't the first, and it won't be the last." Quite unfortunate for the tax payers.

These real-life situations and others like them that you have just read about, do not happen once in a blue moon. In fact, they are usually occurring every time you can see the moon. Policy and procedure. Documentation. Duplication. Little or no accountability. All too common to the system.

Most people do not understand the intricate workings of the system, mainly because they have little or no knowledge of the workers and the roles they play within it. There are many roles being played within the entire justice system, and the D.O.C. is no exception. Jail-house television that the public watches at times gives very little insight to the way it really is. If anything, it tends to either distort it or eliminate many factors unknown to the general public. In all fairness, it is tough to go into any kind of detail in a one or two hour T.V. special or documentary. Drama is the key in those situations, and dramatization often leads to distortion of the true nature of the situation. Don't forget, ratings play a big part in the television world, and the name of the game is to make it exciting so you will want to watch it. I have really only ever seen a handful of shows that are fairly accurate in representing real jail life.

For example, there is a very involved process that leads up to coming to jail. You do not just get picked up one day by a bored or gung-ho police officer and end up in the state prison trying to make your one phone call that the law supposedly allows you. As far as roles being played, the system is known for having a very intricate network of procedures to be followed and personalities to be dealt with. I will try to give you a brief outline on the procedures involving the transformation from suspect to inmate. It should be understood that at each step of the criminal procedure, there are appeals processes, legal exceptions, and technicalities that occur which will not be mentioned in this brief overview. This is primarily designed to give the average reader an idea of the basic proceedings of the legal and incarceratory structures.

First of all, there must be a suspect. The police basically have gotten a call, had a warrant, or seen or heard something suspicious and now they need someone to fit the bill. Whether it be minutes, hours, days, weeks, or years, their job is to make the arrest. Even at this primary stage, once a suspect or suspects have been apprehended, there is a myriad of paperwork that begins to evolve. Essentially what is happening by this time is that a person has been brought in for questioning. It does not mean they are guilty of anything; nor does it mean they have been charged with anything. Some people may ask if they are being arrested at this point; and if they are told no, they may elect to leave by choice. They could then be placed under arrest by law, at which time by due process their Miranda Rights must be read to them. (One does not legally have to be read his rights unless he is being placed under arrest.) Regardless of the time of arrest, one must be read his rights prior to the arrest itself. Also, whether being arrested or not, it is the legal right of all citizens to have an attorney present during any or all questioning, especially for a criminal investigation. Whether one is a suspect or not, regardless of the type of questioning, he retains the right to have counsel present. If one cannot afford counsel, the law entitles him to have an attorney present free of charge. (The Fifth Amendment of the U.S. Constitution protects against self incrimination. Under the Fifth Amendment, the Miranda Rights states: You have the right to an attorney. If you cannot afford an attorney, the state will provide an attorney for you. You have the right to remain silent. If you give up this right, anything you say can and will be used against you in a court of law.)

After questioning, one of two things can occur. Either one is released, or one is booked (placed under arrest). In the case of arrest, which is, and should be, motivated by probable cause, one's Miranda Rights are read, and he is indeed placed under arrest. During the booking procedure, he is fingerprinted, his picture is taken (the classic front and side mug-shots), and more paperwork evolves.

Now, the suspect (who is now the defendant) takes on a

more serious role. He is taken before a magistrate for a hearing. At this hearing, known as the preliminary arraignment, the charges are read, a hearing date is set, and bail is set if applicable. (Bail, by definition in the Pennsylvania Rules of Court manual, is "a monetary security (set by the Judge or magistrate) which is required and given for the release of a person in the custody of the law, conditioned upon a written undertaking that the person will appear when required to do all other things stipulated therein." In other words, a guarantee that one will show up for trial, hearing, or anything else required, without having to remain in jail until that appointed time. It should be known that any bail that is posted (usually in the form of cash or property) is returned, if the defendant does report on time and fulfills the said requirements stipulated. If one does not report and comply with bail stipulations, the bail money is then not refunded, or in the case of property posted as bail, a lien may be placed against the said property. Depending on the nature and circumstances of the crime, the suspect is either held without bail, released under bail terms, or fined and released on his own recognizance. If bail is set but the defendant cannot come up with the money, he is returned to and remains in the county prison awaiting trail. If the charges happen to be more serious, as in first degree murder, for example, a much higher bail is commonly set, if one is set at all. This procedure following the arrest is the prelude to the preliminary hearing.

It should be understood at this time without going into any detail, that the defendant, if represented by counsel, may choose to waive the preliminary hearing and be bound over for court. (The defendant who is not represented by counsel at the preliminary arraignment may not at this time waive the preliminary hearing.) A plea bargain would be one such thing that could dictate this proceeding. Otherwise, if the preliminary hearing is not waived, a date and time is set for the hearing to occur somewhere within three to ten days after arraignment. (Again, there are exceptions to this standard time period which will not be discussed here).

During the next stage, known as the preliminary hearing, the defendant is asked to plead his guilt or innocence: he may call witnesses on his behalf, he may offer evidence on his behalf and testify, he may cross-examine witnesses and inspect physical evidence offered against him, and he may take notes or electronically record the proceedings. It is during this hearing, that a prima facie (something presumed to be true unless disproved) case of the defendant's guilt must be established, or an application for continuance supported by reasonable grounds must be submitted, in order for the defendant to be eligible for trial. If neither of these conditions are met, the issuing authority must then discharge the defendant. If it is decided that the defendant is to indeed be tried, then again, new proceedings must begin to occur.

First of all, the defendant has the choice to be tried by a jury or judge. If he or she chooses trial by judge, the process is somewhat simplified. In proceeding this way, once again, he is entitled to an attorney being present, as in all stages of the legal process, and basically his case is presented to the judge. If he indeed felt at the close of the trial that the judge(s) presiding was unfair for any reason, he may file for a hearing by the whole court, or what is known as a re-hearing En Banc. This is all discretionary by the next higher judge seat.

If the choice is by Jury, the process is undoubtedly more detailed and costly. Naturally, to begin with, a jury must be selected, and can be very costly in both time and money. By the way, I have been told on numerous occasions that many individuals "seasoned" to the system, would and do choose to be tried by "the twelve" (prison slang for jury) over a judge, in an attempt to try and win the sympathy of the jury, and have more opinions rendered. On the other hand, it seems that some who are new to the system seem hesitant to choose a jury, and would rather a judge hear their case due to fear of prejudice and malice toward them or their crime, or in hopes that some sort of deal can be worked out with less time to be served.

The defendant is given the opportunity to enter a plea before the trial even starts, which determines the process from that point. If a trial does indeed occur, two things can basically happen. If the defendant is found innocent of all charges, then of course he is free to return to society after the proceedings are completed. (Assuming there is no other legal restraint or obligation to be fulfilled). On the other hand, if the defendant is tried and found guilty of any or all of the charges, a sentence is then imposed. If the defendant is incarcerated while awaiting trial, she/he must be present for the trial and sentencing to occur. If the defendant is free on bail while awaiting trial, and fails to show up for the trial date, she/he will be tried in absentia. At this point, a warrant would be issued for the defendants arrest, and upon apprehension the defendant will be brought before the court for further disposition of the case.

Once the trial is completed and proceeds to the pre-sentencing stage, if the defendant felt in any way that he was denied a fair trial, he has the right to file post trial motions to include any or all of the previous proceedings in the trial. This must be done before the sentencing if the defendant hopes to raise any further issues or file any further motions after being sentenced. After sentencing, he may file post sentence appeal within ten days of the sentencing date. This then will cover any, and only any issues raised in post trial motions.

Next, after the judge has imposed the sentence, the convicted party is usually returned to the county prison to be held until being sent to the state prison, or in some cases to remain in the county facility to serve his time. (Exceptions to this would be high security or high profile cases, which may be brought directly to the state institution after sentencing.) The judge decides the amount of time to be served, and in some cases the facility where he will serve it. This does not mean that the convicted party cannot or will not be moved during the course of the incarceration. Factors such as discipline, conduct, security, family status, or vocational and educational goals are all conditions for movement to another facility.

In Pennsylvania, if receiving a sentence of up to two years, one generally serves his time in a county facility. Exceptions to this are usually things like high escape risk or high security type inmates for one reason or another. Two years or above in time sentenced will usually place one in a state facility. The exception to this is a person with a federal sentence, or in some cases, where the Judge allows one to serve his state time in a county facility, then to be paroled under the state system. An individual tried and convicted in the federal court system will automatically go to a federal prison to serve his time. This is not to say that he will not come to the state system at some point. If he has a state sentence to serve also, he will come and go between the two systems.

Upon arrival in either type of facility, a whole new process again begins to unfold. The final phase of justice being served, with the exception of the death penalty - incarceration.

Clearly, the paperwork and people involved in these processes is monumental. These processes are set to work in a certain order and time frame. By law, a person is due a fair trial within 180 days of arrest. This time frame is only as good as the staffing to implement it. A few years ago when the jails began filling up at unprecedented rates and arrests and convictions were at an all time high, this 180 day rule became very difficult to adhere to. New extensions had to be granted to accommodate the rising arrest rate, and so led to the existing backlog in the courts today. It is not fair to rush someone through due legal process and risk his rights to a fair trial; nor is it right to have people locked up for undue amounts of time awaiting trial due to court backlogs. Two alternatives exist: increased staffing throughout the court system of competent employees, or a lesser number of criminals. Both ideals seem equally hard to attain. Judges and court officials on the pre-trial end feel at times that the "wheels of justice" need more oil so they may turn more smoothly and quickly. On the other hand, many individuals on the post-trial end that are now looking at incarceration feel that the" wheels" are too well oiled and are moving at such a rate of speed that they have been sped right through without proper attention being given to all the facts and proceedings.

What many people are not aware of today, is that a substantial contribution to certain court backlogs and busy schedules is created by post-trial situations due to improper proceedings during the trial phase. Things such as ineffective assistance of counsel, the exclusion of certain vital evidence, and other improper proceedings on the part of the defense attorney or the prosecution lead to these post-trial days in court. Beyond these situations, are the innumerable appeals that are filed as laws are changed and amended, and as cases are dissected in law clinics day by day throughout the jails themselves. Remember, the hardest and most tedious pursuits some inmates have ever encountered are when they begin researching their own cases for further appeal. And, if they cannot do it themselves, they will seek out a good jail-house lawyer who is well versed in the law. These "jail-house lawyers" are inmates, and every jail usually has a few good ones. These individuals are well versed in many areas of law, especially criminal law, and are well accessed in attaining information when needed. They are very familiar with journals, briefs, and paperwork needed to move throughout the court system.

I know a few personally who have mini - law libraries right in their own cells. Word processors and P.C.'s help to expedite the paperwork and research process. They have spent literally hundreds and hundreds of dollars on reference and law books that walk them through every step of legal procedure. Appeals, briefs, motions, you name it - they can do it. Many of us on the outside world could not afford to hire a legal counsel to do the in depth research and paperwork that these guys do. Payment for these services in jail is dealt with a little differently than it would be outside of prison. A jailhouse lawyer may be compensated for his/her services with items purchased by the inmate(s) from the prison commissary. These items could include cigarettes, toiletries, snacks, or other sundries. Nevertheless, it still costs something, and everything being equal, it is not cheap in some cases.

We have now basically covered the steps beginning with the suspicion and arrest, right up through trial, conviction, and incarceration. Once incarcerated and serving the imposed sentence, inmates who qualify have two options. One situation that is available to certain individuals with appropriate credentials is known as furlow. It allows an incarcerated person to leave the confines of jail to go home for a short time, then return until the next granted leave. Furlow leaves usually begin with a one or two day leave, and at the present time many go up to a seven day maximum stay beyond the prison property. These leaves usually occur over a weekend. To be eligible for furlow, the inmate must be within nine months of his minimum sentence date. The policy used to state that once a person reaches half of his minimum time, he could apply. This changed as of 1994. The inmate must file an application to his counselor as to his desire; then a records check is done. The type of case he has, his conduct while in prison, and his family status are all deciding factors. In some cases, letters or recommendations from judges, district attorneys, or other law officials can definitely negate the furlow status for an individual. The other option open to inmates, again when nearing their minimum sentence, is a condition or status where they can leave the jail property and serve the remaining time of their sentence at home. It is widely used, and plays a vital part in the incarceration phase. It is known as parole.

Parole differs from probation due to the fact that it is part of incarceration. Probation may occur in the pre-trial phase of justice, usually following a guilty plea, or as the result of a guilty verdict in some cases. It is not a sentence of confinement, but rather a condition of release. There is no jail time connected with probation, unless a violation or violations occur, and the judge then decides that jail time is warranted. Probation is usually granted to people who are first time offenders with minor offenses such as retail theft, simple assault or other minor charges, and have no prior record of criminal history. Parole, on the other hand, is basically an extension of jail beyond the actual confines of the building or premises. It is a test of responsibility and desire to be free.

For some individuals, it is much harder to remain on parole than it is to be locked up. As strange as it may sound, it becomes all the more evident day by day to staff working in the jail. On days when we might receive 30 to 35 inmates for example, it is not uncommon that 15 or 20 of these or more are parole violators. Many people accuse the system of failing in the rehabilitative process when examining these statistics. The problem is, that system is not set up to rehabilitate, but to warehouse or "lock away" these "detriments" to society, as some refer to them. The even greater problem that exists is the fact that no where, no how, and in virtually no time frame could the system even expect to make right and reverse all the bad teaching and child rearing that occurred with many of these inmates. Remember, we are seeing the product now, of all the bad examples and teachings at a very young age. The lack of responsibility and self discipline taught at an early age, combined with low self image and immorality are some of the biggest contributing factors. These problems will be discussed further in the chapter on rehabilitation.

In Pennsylvania, the parole system is a very large and encompassing process. Part of this is due to the sheer numbers of people that cities like Philadelphia, Pittsburgh, and various other cities arrest, convict, and incarcerate on a daily basis. The city of Philadelphia alone has dozens of arrests per day, and, in fact, accounts for a little over 40 percent of the total inmate population state wide. As of December 31, 1995, 13,037 inmates or 40.2 percent to be exact - of the total of 32,410 inmates statewide, were from Philadelphia. The second highest contribution to the total that year was from Allegheny County (Pittsburgh and surrounding areas), which totaled 4,137 inmates or 12.8 percent of the total. As these thousands of people yearly come close to their minimum dates of incarceration time, a process begins which allows them to return to their home environment on parole. In most institutions, approximately two to four months prior to the inmates minimum date, they are scheduled to see the parole board for an interview. It should be understood here that not all inmates in the State of Pennsylvania have a minimum and maximum date to their sentence. Life sentences in Pennsylvania are indeed life sentences - one's entire natural life. Unlike other states where even someone with a life sentence is eligible to apply for parole after a certain time, here in Pennsylvania life means life.

Compared to the rest of the states in the nation, Pennsylvania is one of only three that offer no parole eligibility for someone sentenced to life in prison. The other two are Louisiana and South Dakota.

According to a report done by the Pennsylvania Prison Society's Policy and Planning Committee in 1993, there are twenty - two states and the District of Columbia, which have parole eligibility for all lifers. Sixteen other states offer sentencing options both with and without parole for first degree murder convictions. Nine other states offer parole eligibility to anyone convicted of second degree murder, and no parole for first degree murder convictions.

The report indicates that in most of the states with a parole eligibility for lifers, there is a minimum number of years to be served. Some of them may modify the parole eligibility date with credit for good time served. Others adjust the date according to the type of crime committed or the severity. The state of California has what is known as indeterminate life sentences, and then has parole options including mechanisms to change a "life-without-parole" (L.W.O.P.) status. In Pennsylvania, the only way to change a life sentence is by commutation from the Governor of the State, with life parole granted. Another exception would be a new trial, wherein a lessor sentence could be given with a minimum and maximum release date.

Nevertheless, the inmate must have an interview with the parole board and he is asked to submit what is known as a "home plan". This plan basically outlines his plan for re-entering society, and states where he plans to live, who he will live with, and if he will be working and where, among other things. It is always preferable that he has a job secured to go home to, but due to economics and competition for employment, this is not always possible. Right now, according to the Parole Board, approximately 30% of all people leaving this institution (Graterford) and some others, have definite employment lined up upon their return home.

After receiving the home plan, the parole people at the jail forward the information to the parole agent on the street. They will then review the home plan information and check out the situation. They then notify the parole people at the jail of an acceptable or unacceptable situation. This information must then be forwarded to the Pennsylvania Board of Probation and Parole (PBPP) in Harrisburg, and after review, the "green sheet" (so nicknamed due to its color) is sent to the jail where the inmate is housed. The green sheet informs the inmate of his status as far as being accepted or rejected for parole, to which he receives a copy.

If granted parole, the inmate now has a date on which he can legally leave the institution and begin serving the remainder of his sentence off prison property. If he is denied parole, the green sheet states the reason or reasons and gives a date for re-review. Also, if parole has been granted and if the date is close, the PBPP will send the parole release forms along with the green sheet. If it is not close to the release date, the release forms will arrive at a later time closer to that date.

We often hear inmates walking around saying "I'm just waiting on my green sheet." This all-important document is vital to them, since it dictates their future as to freedom, or more incarceration. We also hear them make the statement at times, that "they gave me a hit." This terminology usually indicates that the parole board is requiring them to serve more of their sentence in jail before being released, or a "setback" as some refer to it, on their minimum sentence date.

If the inmate is granted parole, he would then sign the parole release forms, and would receive a copy just as he did with the green sheet. These forms are basically a contract between the inmate and the parole board, stating the conditions to be followed by the parolee.

At the present time, there are seven conditions governing parole, or reparole in some cases, that the parolee is expected to follow. These include any "special conditions" listed in addition to the standard ones, and usually are tailored to each person as needed. Basically, they include (1) Reporting in person or writing within 48 hours of release to the office or sub-office specified, and not leaving the district without the written permission of parole supervision staff. (2) Not changing your residence without the written permission of the supervision staff. (3) Maintaining regular contact with the parole supervision staff by the ways listed on your conditions sheet. (4) Complying with all municipal, county, state, and federal criminal laws, as well as vehicle and liquor codes. (5) Not possessing or selling narcotics or dangerous drugs -or using controlled substances within the meaning of the Controlled Substance, Drug Device, and Cosmetic Act without a prescription. No owning or possessing firearms or other weapons, and refrain from any assaultive behavior. (6) You must pay fines, costs, and restitution imposed on you by the sentencing court. You must establish a payment schedule with the appropriate county authorities within 30 days of your release from prison, for the costs and restitution owed for those cases for which you are now on state parole. While paying these costs, you must provide proof of payment to the parole supervision staff, and inform the parole staff and the court of any changes in your financial ability to pay fines, costs, and restitution. (7) You shall comply with any "special conditions" listed (on second page of conditions sheet). (Title 37 Pa. Code Section 65.4)

There is an option that exists for inmates in a pre-release status, by which they can apply to go to what is known as a Community Corrections Center (CCC). These centers (The first of which opened in 1969), used to be known as Community Service Centers (C.S.C.'s) and provide a place for the inmate to live while still serving time on his minimum sentence, but also trying to phase back into the community at some point. An inmate may apply for the C.C.C. 15 months prior to his minimum sentence date. They must have at least one year left to serve on their minimum sentence before being sent to a center, and if they have no violations during their stay there, they may then be paroled from that C.C.C. It should be understood that the C.C.C. center is actually an extension of jail off of jail property, and not a parole situation just because it is out in the community. There are cases where parolees do live at the C.C.C. once they are indeed paroled, but this is usually just until they can get established and secure housing elsewhere. These are not to be confused with the Community Parole Centers (C.P.C.'s), which serve as "half-way back" facilities for parolees who are having a difficult time under parole supervision. The CPC's deal solely with people on parole, while the C.C.C.'s deal with people on pre-release status who are looking to be paroled.

To apply for the C.C.C., the inmate must basically submit an application to his counselor. Staffing records are then gathered and reviewed, and the institution then will approve or disapprove the application. If disapproved, the inmate must wait at least 90 days before re-applying. If approved, the institution must then notify the sentencing Judge, the District Attorney, and the Office of Victim's Services (OVS) of the intent. Those parties then have 30 days to respond, and if there are no objections, the regional office in the area where the center is located needs to grant the final approval. If approved, the inmate is then notified as to a "bed date", or a date when a bed will be available to him.

Once at the center, if he happens to violate rules while there, he is then returned to the jail proper, and must then see the parole board there to be released. Nevertheless, whether going to a C.C.C. in a pre-release status or going home on parole, the ball is in the inmate's court. It is his decision as to his conduct, which of course decides freedom or incarceration. If he is on parole, the same situation applies as being at a center. A list of rules and regulations are to be followed. If a violation occurs, once again he is returned to the paroling institution, with possibly one stop at a receiving institution in the area, and must have a hearing to review the charge or charges. If he is found guilty of a violation or receives a new charge, what is known as "back time" or additional time to be served in the jail will be decided. It should be understood that the term "back time" does not mean that the inmate is given any more time to serve in addition to his original sentence. It simply means that now, some of the time on the remainder of his sentence that could or would have been served off of prison property, will be served on the prison property. This is usually in conjunction with a violation or new sentence occurring.

Near the end of this back time being served, once again within a certain time frame the inmate must repeat the review process and wait for the green sheet with a re-parole date. There are cases where the inmate's conduct is so bad, and he has so many violations, that he ends up "maxing out" or serving his maximum time in the jail rather than finishing it on the street. There are also some, who by choice, serve their entire sentence in the jail due to their inability to conform to the rules and ways of society, or their vulnerability to return to things and situations which brought them to jail originally. Some inmates returning as parole violators, will blame everyone but themselves for their return. "Techs", or technical violations as they are known, are the most common reason for return. Most P.V.'s do not come back to jail due to a new offense/conviction, but merely a violation of their parole conditions. In many cases, if you did not know better, you would think that the parole people were the worst people in the world to deal with after listening to some of the stories these parole violators tell you. After investigating some of these "outlandish and unwarranted" arrests as we hear them called by some parole violators, you soon find out that a number of warnings and counseling sessions usually proceeded the arrest. Certainly there are situations that warrant the immediate arrest of some individuals without warning, but this is usually the exception, not the rule. The fact is, according to some parole agents I've talked to, that with the large number of people that the parole board must keep tabs on, they have much better things to do than to arrest innocent people all day. The fact is also that inmates generally have a difficult time admitting the fact that they themselves did not take responsibility as far as following the rules, which is usually why they ended up in jail in the first place.

On parole, or pre-release status, conditions- and in some cases "special conditions"-are set for a reason. Inmates are expected to adhere to these, which are usually set due to reasons of past history. For example, if his case involved drugs /and or drug usage, then a stipulation might be that frequent random urinalysis tests can and will be performed. If the inmate refuses, or the results come back positive for a certain drug or drugs, then of course he is in violation. These kinds of conditions are usually tailored to fit each individual, and can encompass things such as living environment, curfew, controlled substance, alcohol, or anything that was or could be a factor not only in his original sentence but in his continued freedom on parole. The parole board is basically the watchdog for anyone who is serving time off institutional property in the parole status. The degree of freedom that a individual has is directly proportional to the responsibility he displays to acquire it and keep it.

The sole function of the parole board is to supervise people serving the remainder of their time off prison property, and not to just try and exert their authority over parolees so they can send them back to jail. In reality, its policies and procedures have, and should continue to teach inmates responsibility, the absence of which led to their involvement with the law to begin with. Had they done so, the parole board would not be so overburdened with people to watch and keep track of.

Clearly, the system of justice that we follow in our State of Pennsylvania alone, encompasses many phases and includes any number of people from the point of suspicion right on through the trial, conviction, incarceration and release of an individual. The manpower and cost generated throughout all the phases discussed in this chapter, multiplied by all the States in our nation, with plus or minus figures due to geographics and population, of course, quickly reveals to us the reason for the prison system along with the justice system as a whole, being one of the largest and fastest growing business in the world today. We cannot build prisons fast enough to accommodate the influx of convicted criminals. Worse than that, the ones we are building sometimes cannot be utilized to the fullest potential due to lack of funds to staff them. And, to add insult to injury, we have not even revealed the costs involved in housing inmates, feeding them, providing medical care, and paying staff members throughout the jails to fill all the positions needed.

In the initial phases of justice served, as discussed earlier, the law enforcement people are the beginning cost factor. Without police, of course, we would all be in big trouble. Then, what about the process that begins to involve the district justice, his secretary, sheriffs for escorts, lawyers for representation, county prisons with correctional officers and medical people, along with maintenance and food service employees, then a judge or judges for trial along with a jury of twelve people with alternates, jury sequestering if necessary (which would entail meals, lodging, etc.) prosecutors, court stenographers, courtroom security people, more escorts for return to jail after sentencing? Then, more sheriffs to escort to the state prisons from the county facilities, and then once in a state facility a myriad of staff to care for the inmate while being housed? This does not even include the parole board and its employees that supervise the inmates upon release, or any other off-site facilities and staff. The list goes on and on.

It is hard at times to convey to people who do not work in the system the magnitude and complexity of what makes the whole thing function. One example I like to use in conversation with people pertaining to the institution at Graterford alone, is mealtime! As of summer, 1999, SCI-G is housing approximately 3,300 inmates. (At one time, Graterford housed approximately 3,500 to 4,200 inmates until more facilities opened up.) We employ approximately 1,200 people. People in general eat three times a day. By these facts, we generate enough food to prepare about 11,000 meals every 24 hours. On a weekly basis, this calculates out to approximately 77,000 meals, which is about 308,000 meals per month. Yearly, this figures out to a little over 4 million meals. Graterford alone spends approximately 4 million dollars per year for food as of 1997.

Another example I like to use is the mailroom. It is not uncommon in a day's time to process 3,000 or more pieces of mail in an eight hour period. Just UPS totals hundreds of pieces per week in addition to all the regular mail. Including personal mail, legal mail, and UPS, the numbers can easily reach 16,000 or more pieces per week during normal weeks of operation. During the holiday season, including regular mail, legal mail and UPS, numbers can easily reach 5,000 or more pieces per day to be handled and processed.

Now to really stagger the imagination, and bring your taxpaying blood to a boil, I will reveal just a few published budget figures to you concerning corrections. The Pennsylvania D.O.C. budget for the 1998-1999 fiscal year is approximately 1.1 billion dollars. The budget for the institution at Graterford alone is almost 88 million dollars for the same time period. These figures have risen by many millions just since the previous year.

Bear in mind, there are a number of jails in the state system that are much smaller than Graterford. There are jails with as few as 68 or 70 inmates, and of course a couple with as many as 3,000 or more inmates. In fact, as of 1999 the system has 24 correctional facilities, 15 Community Corrections Centers (CCC's) and one motivational Boot Camp with approximately 36,500 inmates statewide. Is your collar getting hot? Is the smoke beginning to trickle out of your ears? Well, let me raise your temperature slightly more now and tell you that in 1999 it cost the average taxpayer about $64.50 per day, or approximately $23,500 per year to keep one inmate incarcerated. By comparison, it costs a four year college student in Pennsylvania an average of $12,000 per year to get an education (variables include room and board, type of school, etc.) In 1995, supervision of an inmate on parole was costing approximately $1,427 per year, or about $3.90 per day. The next year, the figure rose to slightly over $4.00 per day, with a projected estimate of approximately $5.00 per day by 1997. According to one source from the office of the Board of Probation and Parole in Harrisburg, this particular statistic is no longer being kept, and the last known estimate that is available concerning parole supervision is approximately $2000 per year, per inmate.

Not surprisingly, the yearly incarceration figure tends to infuriate people whenever they hear it.

To coin a modern phrase, it just makes some people "go ballistic" when they are discussing this issue and giving serious thoughts to these staggering figures mentioned above for keeping people in jail. How long will it be, until we reach a staggering figure of two-billion dollars or more to keep this whole thing functioning ? Not long. Obviously by these cost figures and projections, things just are not getting any better.

So, we build more jails. Hire more staff. Take in more inmates. Build more jails... Hire more staff, ... Wait. Can we really and honestly label this never ending cycle a success? Or is it demonstrating a total failure on the part of the justice system to adequately impede or stop crime in our society?

In reality, prison does play a very important role in the justice system. It basically isolates people for a period of time in hopes of giving them a chance to mature and realize that their way is not the best way, much less the accepted way. The real value of prison is limited, and should be used in conjunction with good programs of rehabilitation, and not as a primary source of making the crooked path straight and moralizing the immoral. At this point in the history of the criminal justice system, the system as a whole has not necessarily failed, but has fallen short in its endeavors to bolster the rehabilitative facet of corrections. We can definitely get them off the street, convict them, and lock them away - we've proven that more than ever before. But now what do we do with them? At some point, many inmates will be returning to society, as bad or worse in many respects as when they came to jail. So the problem has not been resolved, but merely removed for a while, only to return in many cases, as a problem again.

As the business of prison exists today, it is considered to be doing well when it is filled. Its success is judged and is directly proportional to the number of people it incarcerates. To put it bluntly, prison survives on its own failures.

Let us now take a closer look at the actual "house" of conviction and correction-the prison, and those who occupy it.

Sights and Sounds of the "Slammer"

The world of prison offers a real challenge to the senses. It is a very diverse society in which one depends very heavily on what can be seen and heard. The senses of sight and sound help one to know the "feel" of the jail, and helps one prepare to react accordingly to the jail environment from moment to moment.

The fears, dangers, anticipations, and many disappointments that inmates and staff experience daily, are for the most part, calculated as a result of the input from these senses. The sound of handcuffs being closed around someone's wrists, large gates or doors being slammed to restrict movement, or keys rattling loudly as the C.O.'s run to an emergency call for help, all serve as a strong indicator as to what is happening or is about to happen.

Handcuff noise is very common throughout the jail environment, and could simply occur during routine escorts of inmates in a restrictive status. Likewise, all steel doors and gates are loud when being closed, and this noise is not necessarily a cause for alarm. Nevertheless, whether it be loud rattling, keys, closing handcuffs, banging doors, fast moving footsteps or even the hollow sizzle of a piece of smuggled meat cooking on a crude hotplate in one's cell - the sights and sounds of jail should always keep one alert as to what is going on around them.

On the cell block for example, there are radios - many on different stations from each other - that are running at loud volumes, while a wide assortment of television programs compete to be heard.

Throughout the jail, human voices of all tones and volumes fill the already crowded airwaves with a stifling chorus of unmatched lyrics and verbiage. Loud talking, screaming, hollering, yelling, singing, crying, complaining and swearing all contribute to the ever present underlying state of confusion that exists in a jail. Officers heard exerting their authority, and inmates seen both complying and demonstrating rebellion toward that authority. Inmates at times screaming loudly to be heard, and authority figures at times pretending not to hear.

Much to the surprise of many people, sound and noise are very important in jail. In many cases, much more vital than sight. It is the sound of jail that tends to heighten one's senses and alert them to possible danger, and not necessarily what they can see happening. For example, the sound of people running, or guards keys jangling, tends to catch one's attention. Whistles blowing, for something other than chow or work lines, could mean a fight or medical emergency of some kind. The locking or closing of doors quickly on a block, would suggest that something has happened, and inmates are being locked up as fast as possible to secure the jail. A nurse or doctor running onto the block, could indicate a health problem or emergency with an inmate or C.O.. Even inmates running, if not headed for the recreation yard or gym, could signal an incident such as a stabbing for example, has or is about to occur. No matter what the scenario, the sights and sounds of the surroundings are vital indicators.

No matter where, in any given jail there is a definite distinct noise level to those who are accustomed to being there, whether inmate or staff member. A visitor or new employee not used to the environment, might never pick up on those signs, and think that it is business as usual. At any one time of the day, there is a certain noise level considered to be normal.

A lifer of 23 years told me that one of the most outstanding things he remembered about first coming to prison, is the "peace" that falls over the jail about 10:30 p.m. each day. The overwhelming quite and calm that seems to move throughout the prison at this time of night is a constant reminder to him that he has served one more day of incarceration.

In many cases, noise is a good sign. It is when things get very quiet and inmates or C.O.'s are not speaking that one must be very leery about what is to come. Inmates would tend to pick up on this quickly if C.O.'s all of the sudden became "strictly business", with no participation in general prison "rap". Likewise, C.O.'s would tend to become very suspicious and even apprehensive, if average noise levels dropped and inmate conversing dropped to a minimum. When the jail becomes too quiet, much beyond normal settling down levels, the threat or possibility of a bad situation could become a reality.

The "calm before the storm" is a very real indicator, and should never be taken lightly. C.O.'s tend to be very aware, and should be, of this change when it occurs in the jail, and naturally tend to become more alert. Rightfully so, due to the fact that they may be the first target of inmate aggression, simply due to being merely an obstacle in the inmates path - regardless of where they were headed or what they were headed there for. The wrong place at the wrong time so to say. Generally speaking, altercations in the jail environment which involve C.O.'s and inmates for the most part are always spontaneous, and not planned. Nevertheless, the C.O. many times becomes involved in the aggressive actions of inmates simply due to the nature of their job. This is precisely why it greatly behooves them to always be alert and aware of their surroundings.

I can recall a few times over the years, hearing a C.O. or C.O.'s make comments such as "something isn't right, its too quiet." "The inmates aren't talking and movement is slow." "Something's up, a lot of inmates didn't go to work today." "There's more inmates in the yard than usual, a lot of little groups standing around." These almost always preceded lockdowns or actual stabbings and beatings not too long afterward. Needless to say, the sights and sounds that contribute to the "feel" of the jail play a vital part in the daily function and atmosphere.

As for noise, if you could sell it in quantity, it would be a very lucrative business. There is usually so much noise, especially during the time inmates are not locked in for count or bedtime, that it is hard to find a quiet place other than out in the car. Between staff and inmates, noise is as abundant as air at times. but, to those who understand it, it is a good sign.

Upon reminiscing and recollection of my first days and months working in the jail, there are things that remain so vivid that it is just as if they happened yesterday. Some of these "sights and sounds" were and are not just common to jails, but of other environments as well. The element of noise that I just mentioned, or should I say the abundance and level of it, is just one example.

Another such example, was the overwhelming presence of rather large cockroaches that seemed to be present throughout most of the jail. Averaging about one to two inches or more in length in some cases, these hearty little pests were no less than a menace, and thrived on the abundance of food, dampness, and dark places to hide. Every morning as I entered my office, one or two of these little pests were usually waiting for me. On the desk, on the wall, or on the floor, they had a nasty habit of taking flight for a few moments and attaching themselves to my pant leg or my skin if available. Extermination practices back then were not nearly as effective as they are now, if at all, and whatever they were using seemed to make them thrive rather than die. In fact, these were such good specimens, that a biology teacher once asked me to bring him one for display after I described them to him. He said it was the best example of a German cockroach he had ever seen! Nevertheless, these unwelcome little creatures seemed to be as equally or more aggravating at times, then the D.O.C. and the bureaucracy and its ways of operation. The only difference was, the roaches never got under your skin or on your nerves - but had more of a superficial aggravating effect.

Other unpleasant sights common to both civilian and prison life included vermin such as mice (also in my office), rats, bats, and all of their unwelcome offspring. Rabbits occasionally made the prison yard their home inside the wall, while some rabbits, cats, deer, and other wild animals roam free on the 1,650 plus prison acres outside the wall.

Thinking back, I will never forget the ominous sounds of the huge prison gates slamming behind me on the day of my interview, as I entered the strange world of prison and became separated from free society for those couple of hours. These huge iron gates that once allowed clear sight and audible introduction to life behind the wall, have since been replaced with more solid, steel electric doors on tracks, limiting even more the exchange of sight and sound from the free world to the one of incarceration.

I guess the one word that umbrellas most of my memory of that first experience of jail is none other than large. Everything was large. The parking lot, the surrounding property, the huge main gates, the main corridor, the cell blocks, the inmates, the guards, and yes - even the cockroaches! This was the land of the large. Large people, large things, and a large, the largest in the state - inmate population. The largest, most diverse group of people locked away anywhere in the state, for an as equally assorted list of crimes and circumstances.

I recall the first time I witnessed a young white guy who had been assaulted and raped. I can remember the look of pseudo tuff-guy on his face after being told by the inmate that worked with me, that he should cut his shoulder-length hair to avoid looking appetizing to someone with the wrong motive. I also recall the look of fear and tears in his eyes a short time later in the prison infirmary, apparently after the warning had not been taken seriously. He was waiting to see the psychiatrist in an attempt to deal with this unscrupulous yet all too real occurrence in the world of the incarcerated. I believe it is safe to say that these kinds of incidents do not occur as often in this day throughout the jails, but nevertheless are a reality.

While on the subject of sex-related incidents, I have often wondered about the treatment of homosexuals as opposed to heterosexuals. While being a common sight in the jail population, some jails more than others - the holding of hands, kissing, and the wearing of feminine attire and make-up among male inmates and in plain view of correctional officers always amazed me. Even the discovery of two or more people fully engaged in whatever role they chose to play in the relationship is often times overlooked. So be it. But - why then, are normal heterosexual relationships between husband and wife or even boyfriend and girlfriend discouraged and even followed with disciplinary action, in the name of security? (Especially in this day and time, when H.I.V. and A.I.D.S. are so prevalent throughout our society. For the record, the CDC (Centers for Disease Control) stated in 1994, that there were 5.2 cases per 1000 inmates, as opposed to about 0.9 out of every 1,000 people in the general adult unincarcerated population.) It is a known fact, that many beatings, stabbings, and occasional homicides occur in the fight over a homosexual lover or partner, so one

39

might think that these types of situations and conduct would be closely policed while possibly being a little more lenient and accepting of heterosexual activity. Some states even condone conjugal visits, which seem to work well. Nevertheless, I could never understand the limitations placed on normal male-female, husband-wife relationships, while allowing the free expression of other types of sexual activity. Well, so much for sex in jail.

I can recall the "sights and sounds" of my first trip to the old death row, which then housed nine inmates, one to a cell. Occupying nine of a total of 39 cells in the restricted housing unit, a double row of bars separated civilian from convict - the free from the condemned. This was jail at the max - ultimate confinement. Quiet, lonely, isolated, with an overwhelming feeling and sense of permanent separation - at least for this lifetime - 9 men - waiting to die, and praying to live.

By comparison, there are approximately 50 inmates now on death row here at Graterford. No less lonely, no less isolated, and no less apprehensive of what is to eventually come - unless there is a change of law, change of sentence, change of heart on the part of the Governor, or of course - natural death.

I look around and see C.O.'s from time to time who I so vividly remember starting their careers around the same time I started, or sometime after - now some of which are Lieutenants, Captains, Majors, or other administrative capacity type people.

I can vividly recall incidents in which a C.O. or other staff person set up another staff member or members for any number of reasons, and I can remember and relate these situations to a piece of advise I was given by an inmate in the first few days of employment. He simply said, "remember, we are not the only ones you will have to watch here." I later saw the validity in his warning after becoming a victim of it myself, by none other than - fellow staff members. How ironic to think that you could possibly trust inmates - "the bad guys" - more than your fellow workers. By the way, I have only ever experienced this with staff members. C.O.'s might very well experience things like this more often among the inmates and their fellow workers, but I can only speak for my situation.

One other "sight and sound" that I can well remember,

among many, is the sizzle of bologna and hamburgers on a homemade grill, (hotplate), with loaves of bread, cheese, ketchup, mustard, onions, mayo, and butter lined up close by. A mini delicatessen complete with all the fixings, right on the bed in the inmate's cell. My first exposure to one of the best swag men in the jail. (Swag is food and/or sandwiches made by inmates and usually distributed for payment.)

I had walked onto a cell block for the first time, and an inmate that worked up in the infirmary area spotted me and offered to show me how the jail's "better half" lives. (If you can imagine such a distinction among inmates.) As we walked through the block, I was also introduced to a C.O., who I later learned was influential in the guards' union in the jail and happened to be working the block that day. Just a few feet away, much to my surprise, I heard what sounded like the sizzle or "hiss" of meat cooking on a grill, and as I was led through a barrier of curtains at the cell door, there stood the enterprising inmate and his makeshift sandwich shop. At any other given time of the day, the cell converted back to look like just that - a normal cell. Many at Graterford have enjoyed the fruits of this convicts' labor - or should we say, the foods of his labor.

So much for my personal reflections and introductory experiences.

Life among the staff members is pretty much like it would be anywhere else in society. The same general conversation exists, involving family, friends, material objects, vacation plans, education, and world news in general. Women discussing shopping, kids, clothes, and men in some cases. Men discussing cars, money, sports, and women, in many cases. The same general talk common to most work places across the country, and probably around the world. Mixed in of course is the mention of inmates, both good and bad; their crimes, their time, and their talents. Basically, the average employee found anywhere in the work force.

As for life in the cells and on the blocks, a bit more intriguing, but not the least bit desirable to most of us, including inmates. Imagine yourself living in your bathroom at home, if you have an average sized one with a sink, toilet and tub. A room roughly 6 feet by 10 or 12 feet (size varies from jail to jail), which includes a toilet, sink, and one or two beds depending on one or two inmate situations. One small window to the outside, one in the door of a varied size, a few clothes and personal items such as pictures, books and hygiene necessities, possibly a foot locker, and a lot of time to think. This is the space the inmates call their "cell", " home", "house", "hut", "spot", "crib", "pad", "my place" - just to mention some of the terms used. To even stretch the imagination further, just meditate on the thought of spending the rest of one's natural life in that little room, as in the case of lifer's sentenced in Pennsylvania. Short of a miracle, new trial and sentence, commutation, escape, or death, that is one's house for the rest of their natural life. The misinformed public, for the most part, has a hard time comprehending this fact, due to the "early release" rumors they have heard circulating over time concerning people with life sentences.

Of note and for comparison sake, are some statistics indicating the number of lifers incarcerated as compared to the number of commutations, or sentence changes; with the number of execution warrants signed for the period between 1985 through December of 1995. During that 10 year period, which included Governors' Thornburg, Casey, and now Ridge, the lifer population rose steadily from 1,429 inmates in 1985 to 2,973 inmates as of December 31, 1995. During that same period, 34 inmates received a commutation with 23 of them being lifers. In each case, after serving approximately 20 or more years on their sentence, they were able to return to society with the condition of life parole. By contrast, during the same period of time, a total of 62 execution warrants were signed, with two of them being carried out. Both inmates that were executed were in favor, and posted no resistance. (Some inmates have had more than one warrant signed, so there were not actually 62 inmates sentenced to die.) To sum up these statistics, it is evident that almost double the number of inmates that were eventually released from life sentences, were sentenced to die, with two actually being executed. By conventional math, this only adds up to thirty-six people statewide during ten years plus, that were relieved of their life sentence of confinement or execution status by means of commutation or execution. This hardly indicates that "lifers" will be out in a few years after being sentenced, and will return to society, without serving much time for their crime. A total pardon of sentence for a lifer is always a possibility, but consider it for the most part a very, very rare occurrence. So rare in fact, that according to one pardons case specialist that I talked to, if one would or has occurred even in this century, it would be a surprise to him. (When a pardon occurs, the inmate's record is "wiped clean" of any record of the crime or time served on that particular conviction, as if it never happened. This is not to be confused with a commutation, where the sentence is changed, usually to allow the inmate to re-enter society, but with a parole status attached for a period of time up to and including the rest of their life. This is usually the case with a lifer who receives a commutation, and then remains on parole for life, unless eventually they are granted a total pardon.) The normal procedure of release from a sentence of life without parole in the state of Pennsylvania, would either occur through the courts with a modification or change of sentence, through commutation as explained above, or of course, death. A total pardon is surely the exception as of now.

Nevertheless each week, we are receiving people who will make that little room their home for some period of time. It is interesting to observe the environment of a cell, many times reflecting the way someone feels about their sentence, their life, themselves as a person, or the fact that they came to jail period. Just as many of us reflect our lives and schedules by the interiors of our homes, so the inmates do also by the condition of their cells. Some neatly painted, with prison approved rugs on the floor and bed neatly made. Others with paint peeling, food and trash scattered about, clothes and bed disheveled, and a general appearance of non-conformity or bad attitude. Some will tell you they could care less about keeping a neat clean cell, because they could care less about being in jail in the first place. Others are used to living like that in society , so a disorderly cell is no different than home. The roaches and mice love these kinds of people, and will attempt to dominate their environment if allowed. In all fairness, there are a good number of inmates, given the tools and goods, that do take pride in their cells and keep them neat and clean, using paint, rugs, wall decor, and whatever is available during their stay. Keep in mind, that jails may vary in what they allow to be kept in the cell, or what is available to be purchased through commissary. Likewise, the appearance and contents may then vary, but the basics are the same throughout the system. I have seen cells that I could be quite comfortable in - at least for a short time, but the problem is not necessarily staying in the cell with the door closed, but rather the door opening, and having to then face life on the block and throughout the rest of the jail environment.

As you move out of a cell and onto the block, the "bigness" of it all would probably get your attention first. (At least here at Graterford.) With the exception of some of the very small jails, or the dormitory style living in some places, the appearance of dozens, or even hundreds of cells in some cases is stifling to many. In this jail for example, there are blocks with 400 cells, divided into two - 200 cell sections by riot doors in the center. I always compared it to horse paddocks at the race track - lines of sliding doors on tracks as far as you could see. This block size is more common to the older jails than the modern ones now being built. A few picnic tables stationed centrally from one end of the block to the other, tend to invite card games and onlookers along with others just passing time. Large shower rooms, stationed at the center of the block in line with the cells on both sides, provide shower facilities for all inmates on the block. Sometimes very thick with steam and noise, they may become an opportune environment for dangerous incidents to occur. Stabbings, beatings, rapes, or other acts of violence have been known to occur in these limited vision areas, and people who thought they were just going to get clean, may get more than they ever imagined.

As mentioned previously a steady infiltration of noise from radio's, T.V.'s, laughter, and conversation of all levels is usually predominant throughout the cell blocks. With sports being such a dominant interest and pastime in many inmates lives, some inmates tend to place themselves personally into the games.

Many times, they include themselves in the favorite team, and may be heard saying things such as "tonight, we play you" - or "next week, you see us on home court." This is usually two professional teams meeting up, and the inmates take a very personal position with a certain team. Of course, on the off-court or off-field level, the inmate bookies are at work with the gambling and betting aspect of the games. Some inmates are turning big profits from this action, with money and possessions at stake just as on the street. You must pay to play" - and if you don't pay while playing, your playing time could be limited!

The dining hall, again in varying sizes and locations from jail to jail, is another area with dangerous potential. There are a few things important to most inmates and worth fighting for in many cases. Food is one of them. One does not play with a person's meal or their portions if they know what is good for them. Secondary to these, is probably cheating in line to get the grub itself. Even though at times, the chow might be half cooked, half warm, or half palatable, it is still food, and it is still your portion. One quick way to incite a riot in the chow hall is to violate any or all of these areas. With 50 or more inmates in a closed room at once, all trying to get one of the few things they look forward to in the course of a day - a meal - it is a good place to guard your actions and watch your step, literally. Even stepping on a persons toe, could, and has incited incidents. Other than the fact that it is as good as anywhere to start a fight or settle a dispute, it is particularly fertile ground during mealtime.

Almost as fertile as the auditorium during a movie. For those jails that have an auditorium and may show movies on a regular basis, the dark, crowded theater setting is a prime place for trouble to begin. No inmate wants blood on their hands or clothes, nor do they want to be seen on the giving or receiving end of an altercation, so this provides an area where they can "bang and not be banged" so to say. A perfect opportunity to stab or punch with little chance of getting caught. This goes for C.O.'s as well as inmates. Unfortunately, as in one case I knew of, the man was leaving the movie with a fresh gusto for life, but did not realize he was also wearing a fresh blood stained shirt. A stabbing had occurred behind him without him knowing it, and he happened to be wearing some of the evidence. When nabbed by the authorities in the main corridor, the alibi was less than acceptable. When there is a stabbing, and you have fresh blood on your shirt, they just do not want to hear that you knew nothing about it as they are pursuing those who were involved. This is probably why some inmates just do not go to the movies, or want to be anywhere around when the lights go out - even voluntarily! Perfectly understandable.

Another area of particular interest to security is the prison yard. The "yard" as it is known here and most jails, contains a multi-lane running track approximately one-quarter of a mile around, a football field in the center which converts to a baseball field in the spring, basketball courts, multiple weight benches with weights, and multiple handball courts running the length of the enormous prison wall on one side of the entire yard. Does this sound like a large maximum security prison, rather than a sports arena or country club? Absolutely. Does it give one the impression that it could be fun and is not such a bad place after all? Possibly, but it certainly should not. There is nothing here or in any jail that could not be enjoyed at a large health club or exercise facility, without the risk of losing one's life. Running a close second to the dining hall or auditorium, the yard always holds the potential risk of letting one experience their last breath of this lifetime, given the right circumstances. A crowded yard with dozens, or more commonly hundreds of inmates, can be just as dangerous as sitting alone in a cell with the door open. Many stabbings have occurred in prison yards, only to reveal the victim lying in a pool of blood when the crowd cleared. With the perpetrator or perpetrators lost in the masses, the victim can easily be left with no accusers, no evidence, and in desperate need of medical attention, or at worst - funeral arrangements. Tower guards can not see everything, and the aggressors obviously do not want to be seen - so the perfect setting for an act of violence, drug deal, money exchange, and whatever else one could imagine in this type of environment. Many inmates do use the yard for exercise and recreation, but it is certainly not a place to be totally relaxed and taken lightly.

As far as other "sights" within the prison; we here, as do some other jails, have a nice large chapel area helping to meet the various spiritual crisis and counseling needs of the inmates. I personally have participated in and attended some of the services conducted here, and the general feeling and mood is very positive. The stained glass windows, pews, altar accessories, and music all closely resemble any church on the streets of society. Meeting the demands of over 3,300 inmates of all races and religions is no easy task, and I believe it is safe to say that this is one of the more adequately arranged and managed areas. One should never be naive, and assume that the "house of God" so to say, is exempt of all evil doings. Most probably, and hopefully, the most serene and peaceful area in the jail, this chamber of worship has in the past played host to the same ills and problems that exist anywhere else in the prison. Areas of opportunity for sex, drug or money exchange, free phone calls, altercations, or other illicit activity do exist, and cannot be ignored by security due to the fact that it is a chapel intended for religious needs only. It is obvious that some peoples needs differ from others, focusing purely around opportunity, and many have nothing at all to do with "religion".

Another major area of sights and sounds in the jail, usually ringing with the sound of metal plates banging the weight bench, people grunting and yelling, balls bouncing up and down the court, and other associated "sports sounds", is the area we call the field house. The "activities" area of the jail, appropriately named, houses the gym with a basketball court, a weight room, and administrative offices for the activities department. A great place for stress release and exercise combined. Many inmates enjoy going to the field house, since a priority throughout jails for many inmates is staying fit and in good physical condition. The recreation and camaraderie lead to some pretty physical activity, and is not taken lightly by some. Many personal grudges and frustrations are dealt with on the weight pile, basketball court, or football field, and the competitive spirit equals or surpasses any teams or individuals involved in sports on the street. Of particular note, even though located in an area outside the field house, is the boxing ring, where the competition may be equally as great, and is of great interest to many inmates who may have grown up in the city. Some jails even have a paid boxing program, introducing young talent to the field along with seasoned fighters, which lends to some very interesting competition. This area, along with the field house - like any other in jail, lends opportunity to altercations or other incidents, but normally the sports and fitness minded people who use the facilities on a regular basis have one thing on their minds - sports and fitness.

One other area of interest, for a number of reasons, is the visiting room. An area designated for the purpose of allowing inmates to visit with family, friends, lawyers, or other acquaintances. As of now, if an inmate is not under any protective custody such as for disciplinary action, self protection, or capital case status, they may have casual visits with no barriers between them and the visitor. Up until the late 1960's and into the mid 1970's, most jails had a barrier - usually glass or wire screening, that separated civilians from inmates. As time went on, the barriers came down, and visits became more of a casual affair, with hand holding, hugging, and occasional kissing being permitted - or at least over looked at times. In a few states, conjugal visits were approved, for full contact visits between husbands and wives for the most part. Pennsylvania still has not allowed this practice along with most other states throughout the country, and there is no talk of it in the near future that we hear of. Nevertheless, there have been babies made during visits in prison - for a lack of better terminology. Drugs are smuggled in; though small quantities, money is exchanged and gotten back to the blocks, romances are conducted, and occasionally, casual becomes conjugal. It is difficult to watch every move everyone makes, but the C.O.'s usually catch much of the illicit activity that is attempted.

It is interesting to note, that many inmates take offense to other inmates conducting "lewd" practices while in the visiting room, possibly exposing children and other women to the sights and sounds of such activity. It is perfectly understandable how and why this could and does occur, considering the isolation and loneliness that comes with incarceration; but, inmates tend to use a greater level of restraint for the most part while on a visit so they do not risk having the visit terminated, or prohibited in the future. For inmates who get visits, it is a privilege that most do not want to risk losing, so they tend to guard their actions closely. A regular visit for some, could be all that stands in the gap between sanity and insanity, staying or attempting escape, keeping or losing family, or at worst - living or committing suicide. For those who never get visits, of which there are quite a few, the issue is of little importance, yet many seem to be very understanding toward those who do.

While speaking on the subject of sights and sounds in the jail, it would be most unfair to only discuss the physical layout without including the main ingredient of the discussion - the inmates. The element that the public is so curious about.

As for the sights, it is easy for one to look at a group of inmates, and instantly think "yea, they all look like inmates." What do inmates look like? What is so outstanding about their demeanor that would bring about that assumption? Is it the fact that hundreds or thousands of them are dressed alike? Is it the hundreds or thousands of tattoos that are displayed among them, in every conceivable shape, color, size and location? (Tattoos by the way, are usually a stereotype associated with bikers throughout the population, but not all who wear tattoos are bikers, of course) How about the abundance of large muscle mass or the lean, cut physiques of many in the Black race? Is it the unkempt appearance of some, contrasted with the military style and actions of others? Or could it be the pseudo tough - guy expressions often worn by inmates as part of a defense mechanism to keep private - space invaders at a distance? Probably a combination of all the above. Personal dress, physiques, tattoos, beards and hair styles, expressions, earrings (in some cases, through places never meant to sport them), or even a certain gate or way of walking, as to intimidate someone with the wrong motive or intentions. One main observation of inmates that captured my curiosity early on, was the abundance of scars on all parts of their bodies. Many on the back, chest, arms, and faces, these "battle scars" as some refer to them, reveal previous wounds inflicted, and give indication of the environment and lifestyles that many inmates grew up in and were a part of before coming to jail. Stab and slash wounds contribute to many of these scars, with bullet wounds not far behind in number.

As far as inside, X-rays reveal a staggering amount of bullet slugs, pellets, and shrapnel scattered about throughout their bodies. Bullets and fragments lying close to the spine, near the heart, throughout the head and neck and among the extremities, are not uncommon. Shotgun pellets scattered superficially are also very common. Many of these individuals seem to be very resilient, and have had amazing recoveries to their shooting and stabbing injuries. Some even went home or hid out somewhere until they healed up, avoiding the hospitals, Doctor's, and involvement with law enforcement officers. Some of us joke at times about this desire and ability of these guys to survive, and the fact that if it were one of us, we would have succumb to such wounds even with medical treatment. (It has even been said, that one can tell the neighborhood that one is from by the type of scars they bear.) It is amazing what Adrenalin and the desire and need to survive can accomplish.

Such are inmates. All different, but all stereotyped as one entity. As far as sounds, I tend to think of a few verbs that are very fitting. As mentioned earlier in this chapter, a constant tone of loud talking, screaming, hollering, yelling, singing, crying, complaining, and an abundance of swearing tend to dominate the space occupied by inmates.

Such is jail. A giant warehouse, storing every model of inmate known, cataloged by number, and characterized by color, race, and sentence. Moved around for storage as space allows, and summoned for use as the need arises. Some models traded with other facilities, while some remain untouched. A few released after much wear and tear, and others released and returned due to insufficient function. Some exit and remain in "production" (becoming productive members of society), while the remainder convert to warehouse fixtures. As new models arrive and are cataloged for storage, older models are viewed for their ability to withstand the test of time.

And so the cycle continues within this particular "house of

conviction", and others like it. From early morning over crowded breakfast lines, to late evening calm empty corridors. From the eerie, silent, quartz-lit prison yard shadowed by guard towers at dusk; to the noisy, routine arrival of employees during the first few hours of daylight. Employees waiting to get in the gate, and inmates waiting to get out of their cells. Everyone watching each other, but trying to avoid being watched. Employees counting the hours until they can leave, and inmates hoping some day, some month, some year - they might have the same opportunity. The sights and sounds of penitentiary living. The likes of which most people cannot fully appreciate, and most definitely do not want to experience.

Care, Custody and Control

Jails and their powers to be have a real thing about control and protection. Rightfully so. That's their main motive for being in business: protecting society against criminals, protecting staff from criminals, protecting criminals from staff, protecting criminals from other criminals, and, on occasion, protecting staff from other staff - believe it or not.

Control is another thing on which they thrive. Controlling what comes in and what goes out. Controlling who goes in and who goes out. Controlling when - people and things come in and go out. And, on a large scale, controlling the people who control the people and things that come in, go out, and remain in the jail all of the time. This protection and control is of the utmost priority - for obvious reasons - and is known and functions under and by the name of security.

The three C's as we're taught - care, custody, and control - are the main focus of prisons anywhere, or should be, if not so. Number one at the top of the list, above all else, is custody or security. Decisions made minute by minute, hourly, and daily, are based around and upon the security of the jail, the people it incarcerates, and the staff that helps to carry out this vital function.

Security has many gray areas to it when one examines the "secureness" of it all. Security is a word that is used to define the condition or state of being safe - - whether it be important papers, animals, jewelry, people, or any imaginable material objects. It can be used in conjunction with an environment such as home, office, country, body of water, or in this case, jail. Jails are supposed to be very secure places. Secure in the sense that inmates cannot get out, and unauthorized people and things cannot get in. Secure in the sense that civilians are safe while working or doing business inside, and inmates are protected while doing their time. Secure in the sense that employees are not trafficking contraband into the people who are locked away for trafficking contraband - among many other crimes. Secure in the sense that SECURITY runs the jail. A very insecure thought at times, when we consider the mammoth responsibility and task of the security force to maintain and control the unstable, volatile, hostile, ever-threatening environment that exists in jails.

For the most part, the security side of a jail is entrusted to the administration and staff of correctional officers, who are hired to maintain order and control within the jail and its surrounding property. Throughout the State Correctional System in Pennsylvania, the correctional officers make up approximately 65% to 70% of the work force in jails, along with people from administration, correctional industries, treatment, parole, records, maintenance, education, and the medical departments, to name a few. There are a number of employees who work in areas and specialities within these areas mentioned, too numerous to note. Graterford's correctional industry section alone, comprised of the weave, garment, underwear, shoe, and hosiery plants, along with the entire farm staff and freight section employs 25-30 people, and oversees roughly 450 inmate workers. By comparison, there are other smaller institutions in the system that may have only one, two, or a few supervisors overseeing one or two industries and anywhere from a handful on up to a few dozen or more inmate workers. Of course, the larger the jail, the larger the staff. Graterford, Pennsylvania's largest state prison, as previously mentioned, employs as many or more staff as there are total inmates in some jails. It is one of the largest employers in the area, with approximately 1,200 people providing services to and for inmates. The average person, unless exposed to this environment for a period of time, could not begin to imagine the security nightmare that all of this presents.

Security in a jail holds certain similarities to security in a retail store, for example. First of all, we have our security squad, other than the general C.O.'s, that makes it their business to watch employees and their habits. Along with searching cells, searching visitors, searching other employees, and constantly acquiring pertinent information on inside issues, they keep tabs on the actions of their fellow employees. Tips and feedback from jailhouse informants, or "snitches" as they are known, (which by the way, may be inmates or staff) spawn investigations on certain individuals out of suspicion. Internal

Security, as this squad is known, conducts these investigations unknowingly to many employees and inmates alike. One of their sole reasons for existing is to find out how the contraband is getting in and stop it if possible. They take their job very seriously, and tend to stop at nothing to get what they are looking for. One could only wonder what kind of place Graterford and other jails would be if this part of security was not active. It is difficult enough keeping the flow of contraband down with the internal security that is in force, much less if it was cut back or did not exist at all.

In a retail store, for example, security attempts to keep employees and shoppers from carrying things out - - without paying. In a jail, the security force attempts to keep employees and visitors from carrying things in - - and getting paid in some cases. Whether the contraband is being brought in to be sold, used, or consumed by the visitor or employee, it is still illegal. Contraband entering the jail, just like stolen merchandise leaving the store, is an all too common occurrence.

It is a full time job on the part of security to watch the people who have been entrusted with the job of watching and caring for the criminals. Ironically, every time a C.O. or staff member loaded with drugs or other contraband is caught entering the institution, the inmates question who the real criminal is. Some find it amusing. How sad. Who should be watching whom? Of course, if one is of the mentality that one is not a criminal unless he gets caught, and the dollar is the basis for one's waking up every day, then the idea or act of smuggling drugs or other contraband into the jail carries little or no conviction with it - until one is caught. Then the conviction could determine his actions for the rest of his life. Remember, a conviction of mind carries far less a penalty than a conviction by law.

I have seen people suspended for things as minor as over-the-counter headache pills or sinus medication, on up to knives, unreported prescription medications, and thousands of dollars worth of drugs taped to their bodies. Drugs are one of the most common contraband items entering the jail, due to their value once inside. Generally, whatever the street value of the drug might be, in jail it can easily be two to four times as valuable.

Make no mistake about it - - drugs are used and sold in jail every day. If coming in uncut, they are cut, refined, and distributed just like on the street. The tools might be a little primitive or makeshift, but they get the job done. Many times during shakedowns, these items, along with drugs, weapons, and other unauthorized items, are found and seized. When searching an inmate's cell, one never knows what he will find.

People are always curious about how the contraband gets into the jail. Security is likewise curious as to how it gets in. They operate off curiosity. One thing they know to be true is that a certain percentage of employees operate on street mentality rather than on jail mentality. They tend to conceal things in purses, coats, socks, shoes, glove fingers, pockets, or anywhere else that is dark and hidden. Mouths, rectums, and other body cavities certainly are not beyond suspicion. In fact, there is a separate little room located at the main entrance of the jail just between the first two security gates as you enter, that was designed with these things in mind. What many employees forget, or just are not aware of, is that at any time and as many times as desired or warranted, they can be searched. They may be called into that little room and checked out right down to the proverbial birthday suit, if need be. Of course, there is policy and procedure written for this also, which governs who is to be there and how the search is to be conducted.

Many interesting items have been discovered during some of these searches performed both at random, and by choice, due to information which caused suspicion. In times past, there have been a number of embarrassed employees that have been escorted out of the institution to a waiting State Police car due to things such as drugs or weapons being concealed. Of course, not all people caught with contraband are handed over to the State Police for prosecution. In most cases, during routine searches, employees may have simply forgotten to take things out of their pockets or purse that are everyday items to be carried by all of us, and thus are asked to either take them out to their vehicles or just discard them before entering the jail. Things such as checkbooks, credit cards, maps, nail polish, chewing gum, or too much cash would fit this category. Though these are not illegal items to conceal or carry in everyday life, they are considered contraband once entering the jail because of the various uses they offer. Most of us who have worked in a jail for any length of time are guilty of forgetting and walking in with items such as those mentioned, and usually are quickly reminded of the policy concerning contraband in the jail.

I can vividly recall how difficult it was just getting myself in at times when I first started, let alone something that was not supposed to be coming in. Institution policy at the time was to not issue an I.D. badge to any contract employees, of which I was one, which then later was changed to issuance after probationary period was completed. Consequently during that time, one just hoped that the C.O. working the front gate had a good memory for faces, or leaving the jail could be as hard or harder as getting in. There were a number of days, when I stood at that large iron bar gate waiting for someone who could justify my entering the jail. Likewise, and even worse, there were many wasted segments of time and thoughts of not leaving, due to a change of shift and no familiar face to release me once again to the free world. It was those moments that caused me to begin wondering what it must be like to not be able to leave and in some cases, forever.

With this procedure as it is presently, scenarios like this would rarely, if ever occur now. All employees, state or contract, are issued I.D. badges from the start, and are checked on a regular basis. As for visitors entering the jail to conduct business (other than the visiting room), a sign-in sheet is completed and initialed by the gate officer, a temporary I.D. badge is issued to be worn above the waist and in plain view, a band is placed on one wrist, and one hand is stamped with a florescent ink that must be viewed under an ultraviolet light. Hands of visitors coming to see inmates are also stamped using this same method.

Likewise, when the visitors are ready to leave the jail, the hand is again checked, the badge is returned, the band is cut off by the gate officer, a form of I.D. is checked (i.e. drivers license, etc.) and the visitor signs out as the gate officer watches and then initials the sheet once again to verify that they allowed the visitor(s) to leave.

There are visitors that come to jail daily to visit inmates other than those who may come in to conduct business, repair machinery, or to work with construction crews doing renovating or building on the property. This introduces a whole different spectrum of people that would be of concern to security. As far as visitors coming to see inmates, a certain procedure is followed to help ensure general security. Things such as purses, other than small change purses, brief cases, umbrellas, combs, beepers, or any of the previously mentioned items are prohibited. There are lockers located in the entrance area of the jail that can be rented to secure these or other items until the visit is over, and then the rental money is returned to the visitor after the visit is over.

According to D.O.C. and Institutional policy, money in the hands of inmates is contraband in jail. If it is indeed passed to the inmate and found in their possession, a reprimand of course is enforced. Misconduct reports, hearings, and disciplinary measures all accompany such actions dealing with contraband. To help prevent this exchange of money on visits, all of the vending machines for food and drink are designed to accept tokens, which can be purchased by the visitor before entering for the visit. In years past, a specific amount of money was permitted to be taken in by the visitors and used in the currency vending machines, until recently being converted for token use only.

Upon entering, the visitor basically goes through the procedure that employees do when coming in. They are asked to remove everything from their pockets and all accessories such as watches, and must walk through the metal detector. There is also a scanner being used now, which was introduced into the screening procedure in the early part of 1996. This scanner can detect the presence of a controlled substance such as marijuana, cocaine, or other drugs, if such a person has come in contact with such substances. If no suspicion arises on the part of security, as in the metal detector or scanner going off, they can then gather their belongings and move into the visiting area as the electric doors allow access. Once inside the visiting room, they meet up with the inmate, who by then has changed clothes and is wearing a pair of pants and shirt used only on visits. Visiting room clothes are usually a different color than any other prison issue clothing, and easily detectable outside the visiting area. It is important that inmates are able to be identified quickly to help prevent escapes by changing clothes with someone in the bathroom, for example. I can remember one time when this very thing occurred with two brothers. Fortunately, now, security measures have been updated and improved, making it increasingly difficult to escape by this method.

Likewise, when the visit is over, the inmate must change again into his regular prison attire before leaving the visiting area. Inmates are required to strip before changing clothes to enter the visiting area, and upon leaving, all inmates are asked to strip again, and a visual search is conducted, including a search of body cavities. The inmate, once clearing the search, may then dress and return to the cell block or wherever they might have to go. In all honesty, it is more difficult for an inmate to transport contraband from a visit, especially of any sizeable amount, than it is for an employee to come in the front gate with it. The constant speculation and rumor that much of this contraband is coming into the jail through the visitors is simply not true. One tends to wonder, with all these security measures in place, how the large amounts of contraband are still getting inside the institution.

Granted, there have been circumstances where drugs have entered the jail concealed between the layers of a baby's diaper, for example, or a concealed balloon or balloons filled with cocaine or other substances have been discovered during a visit, but these occurrences usually are more geared toward personal use rather than re-sale or distribution, and are small quantities. Unfortunately, there have been scenarios like these that ended in a fatality due to a balloon rupturing in the stomach of the inmate before he could recover it, with the entire contents entering the body at once, or a voluntary overdose after returning to the block. These are not every day occurrences, but rather once in a while happenings. This also reflects on the competency and efficiency in the security staff as far as intercepting and stopping the flow of drugs and contraband from visitor to inmate.

Unfortunately, it is much more difficult with staff, by reason of large roster, job site, and time schedules, to monitor all the actions and movement in a days time. As the staff moving in and out of this jail greatly outnumbers the total visitors within a 24 hour period, so do the chances of contraband coming in by employees, versus visitors.

In jail, as in any other business, it is always easier and more convenient at times to shift the blame to outsiders, rather than admit to and expose the ongoing and often glaring problems that exist internally. Then of course, even once the offender or offenders has become known, nabbing them with the goods in their possession is the other problem. Security is usually quite certain of possession when confining someone between the gates and making a major issue of the search. These types of searches differ a bit from the routine "step-over-here-a-minute" searches conducted as you are reporting for work. As mentioned earlier, a tip from a knowing source usually leads up to the searches that expose significant contraband in type and amount, whether it be drugs, weapons, or large sums of money. Make no mistake about it - - if you are smuggling contraband into the jail in any sizeable amount and for any length of time, your chances are very good of getting caught. If the motive is revenge, especially on the part of an inmate, the trafficker is sure to be exposed. It is a well known fact that some inmates would not hesitate a minute to set someone up to be caught out of dislike or revenge, and in some cases the employee might be a first or infrequent time offender as far as contraband. This is precisely why all employees are told from the very beginning not to have any business dealings or personal dealings with inmates. Contrary to some employees beliefs, these rules are not made to segregate and isolate inmates from civilians, but rather to procreate a professional and safe environment among inmates and employees throughout the jail. Time tested experience has had major input in the formation of many policies that exist in the jails, and prime offenders who are trafficking drugs or other contraband would greatly benefit by not using inmates to supplement their income, lest they eventually come to occupy a cell themselves.

This brings us to another facet of security within the jail that is probably the most time consuming, tedious job within the system involving correctional officers - - the inmate housing and work areas. Cell after cell, block after block, jail after jail. Seemingly endless areas to watch and keep track of day after day, week after week, month after month, year after year. A continual maze of storage and hiding places for objects and people. Scores of items to monitor and masses of people to patrol. Quite naturally, the bigger the jail, the bigger the job. Televisions, radios, books, beds, shelves, foot lockers, toilets, sinks-all potential hiding places for contraband. Cells have been known to contain as little as one marijuana cigarette, or up to dozens of cartons of brand types that are available in the commissary. By policy, there are limits to the number of things you may have in your cell such as cigarettes, clothing, etc. Unique items such as small stills for making "jailhouse wine", or foot lockers that convert to ovens and vent to the outside for cooking whole chickens have been uncovered. Objects known as "stingers", made from a piece of electrical cord and plugged into an outlet for heating water are common finds during shakedowns. False-back shelf units and cabinets contribute to the never ending list of ingenuous hiding places used for contraband. Tattoo needles, dyes and inks, drug works, syringes, and hot plates are among the never ending list of illegal items that turn up. Large trash cans on the cell blocks with a normal looking bag of trash under the lid, may conceal a few gallons of homemade wine in another sealed trash bag in the bottom of the can. Normal looking fire extinguishers have even been known to have been drained of their water and used as storage containers for wine. A fire never had it so good!

Quantities of money, ranging from a few dollars on up to hundreds or thousands of dollars, have been uncovered in socks, books, walking canes, or bed mattresses, and come in quite handy when gambling or betting, which opens the door in many cases to debt. A common problem in jail, but undoubtedly one of the most dangerous. Whether it be a pack or two of cigarettes, other commissary, a favor, or gambling debt, it can and does escalate into a life and death situation if not settled. Many times it is not the actual item, but the principle of the thing. Debt in jail leads to beatings, stabbings, and sometimes death. In many cases, these incidents are performed with weapons fashioned by inmates and made from anything imaginable, ranging from a single ink pen to a custom made dagger or sword.

Homemade knives - - shives, shanks, wacks - - called by whatever name, are undoubtedly the most common item to be found during searches, with drugs running not far behind. Lengthwise -- I've seen them as short as three or four inches, and as long as two to two and one half feet in length, and everything in between. Blades sometimes measuring one to one and one half inches wide, on down to sharply polished ice picks. Handles taped and formed for the best grip, and in some cases even a carrying case to provide protection and concealment as a holster would for a gun. Whether they be pieces of a bed frame, bars from a window, a metal stem from a sink faucet, or a random piece of steel or plastic from machinery in the industrial shop, they turn into a potential instrument of crime and are very deadly once sharpened and completed.

Even a common padlock, sold in the prison commissary and used for cell doors and foot lockers, can be a deadly weapon when placed in a sock and swung around like a crude slingshot to hit someone. The "lock - in - a - sock", as it is referred to, has been used many times during a confrontation to "split a guy's wig" as prison slang has it, thus placing a sizable laceration or even dents in ones' skull or other accessible areas. A display is set up from time to time - most often after a major shakedown, revealing various weapons and contraband that were confiscated in various areas of the jail, usually housing areas for the most part. These displays, designed to enlighten employees of the craftiness and wide variety of contraband typical to a jail, tend to send out a message to the civilians that inmates are very serious about security -- their own, that is. Just as many inmates carried weapons on the street and did not depend on police for protection, so it is in jail. By far, not all inmates carry weapons or store and use contraband, but many have easy access to these items if the need arises. Whether it be a shank or syringe, a certain drug or dollar amount, it can usually be gotten in jail.

A worst case scenario involving weapons could resemble the incident that occurred at Graterford in the fall of 1981, when a group of nine men, four of which were armed, attempted to escape by going over the wall. Early one evening, an officer in one of the towers spotted the group of men with the homemade rope ladder and other articles attempting to scale the wall, and moved out onto the catwalk and warned them to go back. An exchange of gunfire occurred, and as other officers were approaching them on the ground, they retreated back to the building, consequently taking six staff members and 32 inmates hostage. Having the weapons still in their possession, the potential for tragedy was all too real. The incident dragged out over five days until the inmates surrendered peacefully. Fortunately, no one was harmed. (I recall this incident very well due to the fact that just three hours prior, as mentioned before, I had been in the jail for the first time in my life for a job interview. I would love to give you all the details of the incident, but that is really not the issue at this point.) The issue, in reality, is everyone's worst nightmare who works in a jail day after day, regardless of location - inmates having guns and taking hostages. This leads us back to the ongoing question - how did the weapons get into the hands of the inmates?

So, did this incident leave me with a feeling of security about inmates and the "secureness" of a jail? Yea, right.

The term "security", to most of us in general, usually accompanies the thought or association of locks, keys, and safety. In our personal lives, things such as dead bolts, padlocks, alarm systems, keyless entries, and video monitoring systems help to protect our homes, cars, boats, and other prized possessions from intruders. Jails are much the same, but on a much larger scale of course. Keys, locks and monitors play a very vital part in jail security. Graterford happens to be equipped with approximately 8 million dollars worth of locks, both electrical and mechanical. Some door-lock combinations, as we have installed on the new side of the jail, are generally in the neighborhood of $6,000.00 each. Multiply this by 500 cells alone, and one arrives at a hefty figure of 3 million dollars. Accompanying these, of course, are the electrical control panels loaded with buttons to open and close cell doors, block doors, and corridor doors. Throughout the older part of the jail, the mechanical locks are still being used on cells, block doors and all doors leading to the areas within the building. Cell doors contain two mechanical locks each, which multiplied by 2,000 cells gives one a 4,000 lock headache. But it doesn't stop there. For every mechanical lock, one needs a key. For every electrical lock, one needs an override key. Between the keys and the copy machines, the normal daily operating procedure seems to hinge solely on paper and brass - - with a number of human beings integrated to coordinate and carry out the effort!

Daily, as we enter the jail to perform the assigned duties, many of us stop at one of the control centers located in the main corridor and trade in a small metal or brass tag with our name on it, in exchange for a set of keys. These keys allow access to the area or areas everyone may work in, and are limited in their function. Each set or ring of keys is designed with a certain function in mind. This helps to limit access to areas one does not work in, or does not belong in. If one needs access to another area, an authorized person is usually available with the needed key. This is one way, and the main way, that security can effectively limit movement throughout the jail, and prevent unnecessary occurrences and incidents, whether by inmate or employee. Incidents such as thefts, assaults, and escapes are kept at the very minimum due to this vast and ever improving key and lock system. This intricate system, however, does not come cheap. Along with the previously mentioned cost figures, this key assortment and arrangement has an approximate value of $500,000.00 to $750,000.00 or more!

When I heard these facts originally, I sat in amazement. The key vault alone, which houses one of a kind keys and master keys, contains about $60,000.00 worth of this precious metal. Considering the fact that some larger keys can cost $30.00 to $40.00 each, and of which there are many, then these numbers do not seem impossible.

For those of us who carry keys all day long and interact with inmates on a regular basis, guarding these keys is essential. All that is needed in most cases is an impression, or even a good look, and a working copy of a key can be made by an industrious inmate. Many exact working copies or almost finished copies of block door keys and other large area keys have turned up during cell searches and shakedowns. Made from metal, plastic or other hard objects, these copies usually work very well, and are kept for just the right opportunity to be used, unless discovered and confiscated first. Inmates, in the past, have been known to move freely in and out of an area using a handmade key, or just wait for that one right moment, whether it be weeks, months, or longer. Precisely why employees who carry keys are urged never to lay them down on a desk, table or other flat surface where an inmate could lay their hand on them to make an impression, only to be traced with a pen or pencil and later used for a template. Or, worse case scenario, the inmate just picks up the keys and leaves, both of which can and has happened.

When employees who carry keys leave the jail, for whatever reason, all keys belonging to the institution must be turned in. Again, so that security can keep track of the keys, and prevent duplication by someone other than our locksmith. A very crucial item in maintaining security in the jail -- so crucial, that if an employee leaves the property with a key or keys, especially that control a vital or high traffic area, they are expected to terminate the ride home, or to the shore, or wherever they are headed, and return them immediately. The officials do not want to hear that you will drop them off sometime in the next day or two. Unfortunately, some of us have made that mistake, and begrudgingly but willfully driven all the way back again in the same day and returned them. This is not too bad a mile or few down the road, but five, ten, fifteen or more - (you get the picture).

Security, especially in a jail this size, has an absolutely monumental task. As you have just read, the endless avenues for the entrance of contraband, the making and storing of weapons, the use of weapons, the violation of policy by employees, and the many ongoing investigations surrounding all these situations involving inmates and employees alike are, nonetheless, tedious and time-consuming. Security within the jail begins with each and every individual. Employees are constantly watching inmates, and inmates are doing the same to employees. Like spy vs. spy -- who is watching whom? Who is trying to outsmart whom? With each and every breach of security, the level of security decreases both individually and collectively. As security decreases due to laziness and irresponsibility on the part of the employees, the risk factor for bodily harm and escape by inmates continues to rise.

I like to remind people on the outside who are not versed in prison policy and procedure, that guns and clubs are not carried by guards and security personnel inside the institution, as television jail sometimes portrays. In fact, the only guns or weapons found to be used are either in the small weapons and ammo room near the front gate, the gun towers which surround the building and prison yard, or in the vault where weapons and ammunition are stored for use by the Correctional Emergency Response Team (C.E.R.T.) as it is known. Naturally the storage of weapons, guard tower positioning, and use vary with each institution, but policy concerning weapons in the jail is the same. There is not a state institution within Pennsylvania in which you will see guards walking the blocks or corridors with loaded shotguns or nightsticks like television jailhouse tends to show. There is enough sensationalism here without the added feature of loaded weapons in among inmates. Be assured most inmates are usually always ready to meet a physical challenge, and in most if not all jails guts would greatly outnumber guns. On a cellblock with 500 to 700 men, and even ten guards on a good day, each officer armed with even two guns fully loaded would not begin to stop an entire angry, fast moving block of inmates from overpowering the guards taking keys, and continuing on their way. They might stop a few, but by sheer numbers they are already defeated. Then, of course there have been guns and keys in the hands of inmates, and worst case scenario -- hostages. At that point, the inmates have all the power, and are calling the shots. If they choose to, they can move right up to the front gate, taking more hostages and injuring at will. When something like this occurs, even on a smaller scale, the inmates have control of the jail, not security. This is obviously the nightmare of any warden or superintendent, as happened at the State Correctional Institution at Camp Hill back in 1989. Some jails across the country might, and in fact, do have the physical and administrative layout which allows weapons within the jail proper, but not so here in Pennsylvania.

Another dimension of security entails the more obvious sight to anyone driving by or up to the prison, and that is the fence or wall which surrounds the jail itself. Here in Pennsylvania, three of the older jails which are all basically maximum security, still have the large, towering thick walls that surround the main part of the jail. The walls, being solid, re-enforced concrete, stand approximately 30 to 40 feet high, with nearly the same length of massive concrete extending below the ground. For the escape minded inmate, that is a lot to climb and even more to dig through or under. Guard towers span the monstrous wall at interval distances all the way around. At Graterford for example, the officer ascends to the top of the tower via a winding staircase, and remains there until relieved by the next shift. They eat, observe, and even relieve themselves in that small room surrounded by windows for observation, occasionally walking out on the catwalk along the wall for a better look or a little exercise. In a small room 40 plus feet off the ground, for eight hours, befriended by a phone, toilet, sink, chair and guns, you appreciate a total different side of security as opposed to working the employee or pedestrian gates, or a cell block. As someone once said jokingly, but with pun intended, "not necessarily a higher level of security, just a more lonely one."

Most of the new jails being built or converted from a previous facility are now surrounded by fences. Usually double or triple fence with space in between, they are topped with barbed or razor wire, and allow visibility to the outside world from within the prison confines. Many critics argue that this new appearance tends to lesson the severity and impact that jail had on people years ago, and that the confinement is "less confining" now to those imprisoned. Some rehabilitation experts argue that it is good not to totally cut off the inmate from the outside world, but by being able to see freedom, it will give them something for which to hope and work. I strongly believe that rehabilitation and inmate self-worth and ambition are not on the forefront of thinking when designing and confining to a construction budget. In the society we live in, the dollar usually dictates design, and jails are no exception. Regardless of any rationale given, pro or con, believe this -- fences are monumentally cheaper to erect than concrete walls, and that's why they are the confinement of choice. Or as someone once said: "High fences are fine, but I think hungry dogs or tigers running in between would markedly heighten the effect, while still allowing the inmate clear vision." Interesting concept.

So in summary, security - at least here at Graterford - exists around the perimeter of the jail by means of the reservation patrol and the large wall. When entering the jail, by way of electric gates, metal detectors and drug detection devices are monitored and operated by officers for both employees and visitors. Security exists inside the jail by way of correctional officers and internal security measures. As of 1996, K-9 dogs were introduced throughout the system in an attempt to help find drugs hidden throughout the jails and surrounding property. Officers man gun towers 24 hours a day, watching activity on both sides of the wall. Restricted housing units, or R.H.U.'s as they are known, are for isolating inmates for self protection, or who are a threat to themselves or others, or both. Guards can even double-lock inmates in their cells and feed them there for the same purpose. (The term double-lock is used merely because there are two locks on each cell door, and both are locked in this case.) As in the other jails throughout the state system, the C.E.R.T. team, as previously mentioned, is available to quell potentially dangerous situations hopefully before they get out of hand. To augment that level of security, the State Police are of course available 24 hours a day to respond if a situation does become uncontrollable. Riot gates are positioned at different areas from one end of the huge main corridor to the other, which itself is approximately one quarter of a mile long. There are riot doors that divide all the large cell blocks in half to insure better crowd control and restrict movement, especially during an incident.

Shakedowns, in which cells and other areas of the jail are searched, are performed routinely throughout the year, for the purpose of eliminating contraband throughout the institution. These are, of course, only as thorough as the officers performing them. Incidents have occurred in the past shortly after shakedowns that involved homemade weapons of sorts, and one even exhibiting a ball-peaned hammer, which was used to place a nice dent in another man's skull. These are the situations that are hopefully prevented but occasionally and unfortunately do occur. Employees can all be potential targets of this aggression by inmates, and must never forget where they work.

Security is first and foremost in any jail. It takes precedent over any other function that occurs. Besides all the mechanical and structural factors working properly, the human element must function as a finely tuned piece of machinery to complete the process. The issue of security in a jail setting is an individual, yet all encompassing concept. It begins with each and every person as a single, voluntary factor, and ultimately permeates every door, key, lock and wall. These jails of correction-the physical buildings, and methods of human restraint-are only as effective and security oriented as the people empowered to use them.

A most blatant example of this occurred on January 8, 1997 at the state's oldest facility at SCI-Pittsburgh. It demonstrated what can, and in fact did happen, when prison staff becomes complacent about security practices within a jail, allowing six inmates to escape and have hours to travel before they were discovered missing. Adding insult to injury, prison officials then failed to notify city police for hours after the escape due to a mix-up.

According to a 117 page D. O. C. report released by Governor Ridge's office, the 115 year-old prison had some problems that went uncorrected for nearly 45 years. It stated that many of the existing problems that contributed to the escape, were also existing at the same time that 10 inmates escaped in 1952, and were listed in a report published about the prison in 1953.

In the most recent escape on January 8th, inmates had access to and were in possession of power tools, extension cords, digging equipment, and blueprints and schematics of the entire prison and its alarm systems. The report states that tool control was "virtually non-existent" in most areas of the jail. Stolen keys were used to gain access to a crawl space that led to the tunnel that was dug for the escape. One of these keys was even found in an inmates cell after his escape.

The report outlined how inmates were left to work in areas throughout the jail for hours at a time without supervision. It mentions the fact that inmates worked excessive overtime throughout the night, and were supervised by an outside contractor who was hired to replace steam pipes, using inmate labor instead of civilian labor. Inmates routinely had access to telephones and fax and copy machines in the maintenance areas. The blueprints and schematics of the entire institution were kept in unlocked cabinets.

It mentions one employee assigned to the maintenance shop, who had keys for areas without permission. On occasion, the employee would allow an inmate into a locked area that led to the crawl space where the inmates escaped from. It also mentions one employee who failed to report that his two-way radio was missing the day of the escape. That radio was believed to be used in monitoring activities in the prison during the escape.

The report states that the inmates tunneled under the prison wall to the outside warehouse, used a stolen hydraulic jack to crack through the concrete floor, changed into civilian clothes, and left through a door onto the street. The warehouse has an alarm system with motion detectors, but was inoperable at the time of the escape. Their escape would have been detected had the alarm system been working.

Inmate counts at the prison were often inaccurate due to inmates being permitted to remain at work or other locations during the count. Unfortunately, the realization of the escape was not known for several hours due to delays associated with the inmate counts. This method of operation, along with several other policies and procedures, has been changed since the escape. Changes in policy and personnel are also being made in other institutions around the state as a result of the escape.

In conclusion, the report stated that "the escape was preventable, and occurred because security at SCI-Pittsburgh was inadequate and contrary to state policy." "The security lapses were not isolated events; rather, they demonstrated a historical and continuing failure to institute meaningful security precautions and procedures."

This is obviously one of those occurrences that could have been prevented if proper policy and procedure were being followed. With the proper efforts of the staff, an escape such as this would have, and should have been impossible. When security becomes negligent and lax in its day to day function, anything can be expected.

It should be understood that some of the people who are incarcerated obviously do not wish to be so; nor do they feel that it is justified due to injustice or other self justification relative to their particular circumstances. Some inmates also tend to constantly display attitudes and actions conducive to lawlessness, irresponsibility, and irrationalism, thus making it very difficult and challenging to introduce an order of security and balance into the prison environment.

On the other hand, speech and actions are as vital in a jail as locks and keys - if not more. Prison workers should think before they speak and act, so as to avoid the consequences of just reacting. Small arguments or the exchange of a few words can and have escalated into an all out physical fight with weapons in some cases, due to the lack of wisdom and common sense being exercised by a C.O. or other staff member - - or more commonly the inmates that are involved. Careless or hostile words, along with spontaneous thoughtless actions, can turn a seemingly secure environment into a riotous one within a matter of seconds. Statistically, most riots are spontaneous, not planned. Many situations begin with only two people, and escalate very quickly to involve many. Likewise, there are times when one person meant the difference between an incident being defused or the whole cell block going up in smoke and lives possibly being lost.

Jails by far would be more secure places for both staff and

inmates if common sense were common practice. First and foremost, employees should be the ones to set the example, making a constant effort to try to defuse the already hostile and volatile environment that exists, whenever possible. A little common sense goes a long way in the everyday confrontations that occur in jail. All facets of security are vital in a jail. A rational, even-tempered correctional officer is just as vital as the large steel door or gate that locks behind him. A staff member who guards his keys from getting into the hands of an inmate is just as important as the C.O. in the gun tower who has good aim. Different people and equipment, different situations, at different times - - all vital to the total security of a jail. Remember, some of the best tools for any job are not necessarily those that cost the most or bear a certain brand name, but rather those that are used with skill, ability, experience, and imagination. That includes the human element as well.

In conclusion, one might ask, is prison really a secure place? Are inmates really secure in prison? Are employees really secure within the prison confines?

Is free society secure in its assumption, that inmates probably cannot and will not be able to escape, and that proper measures are being taken to prevent such occurrences?

Questions such as these are answered everyday, by the evidence of the collective efforts of those to whom the jails's operation is entrusted, and their dedication to none other than - care, custody, and control.

Prison Inhabitants

Inmates, cons, convicts, residents, prisoners. All labels for the same product. Cunning, creative, ambitious, discerning, perceptive, ingenious, manipulative, talented, intriguing. All in an attempt to describe the diversity of prison population. Incarcerated individuals who say they are prisoners of the system. Regardless of the label, they are people who have been tried and convicted of a crime or crimes and subsequently sentenced to prison.

Among the incarcerated, there are those who profess their innocence. This protestation of innocence more often than not is based on their own interpretation of the law. Remember, the circumstances relating to a crime do not change or alter the fact that a crime was committed. Circumstances only tend to enhance or lessen the severity of that crime. These are known as aggravating or mitigating circumstances. Aggravating being things that contribute to the severity or intent of the crime, and mitigating being things that tend to lessen the severity or intent of the crime.

Some people have convinced themselves that if they did something illegal and got away with it, then it was no crime. Many incarcerated individuals fall into the trap of deceiving themselves on this issue. It seems to be a common factor in street mentality to be the deceiver rather than the deceived. This is not to say that being deceived is good, or that we should incorporate it into our lives as a substrate of humbleness. Many inmates practice deceit as an aggressive role in their individual lives. Many feel that to deal with the system and get what they think they need, they must "get over" on someone, or "dupe" them to accomplish some goal that they have. Quite naturally, this puts civilians on alert all the time when dealing with inmates, thinking that the inmate is "working them" or up to something. It becomes quite natural to be suspicious of someone when working in the prison environment. Let's face it, when you are placed in an unnatural environment such as jail, you tend to do whatever you must to survive. Now couple that with the street smarts that many of these inmates acquired at a very early age, and you see where the term "con man" comes from. Always trying to get something from someone or somewhere, that they either are not entitled to have or cannot easily get, even if they are supposed to have it.

The system provides many detours on the road of accessibility of things to inmates. A missing signature, a missing number or date, an unclear order - or an employee who does not feel like doing their job on a certain day, all help to contribute to impediment of the process.

Regardless, the system does provide the basic needs of inmates such as food, clothing, shelter, and a bed. Medical care is provided (at no cost to the inmate at the present time, but pending legislation, if adopted and enforced as anticipated in the near future, would require some inmate contribution for certain medical services rendered). It also provides recreation if one desires to take advantage of it. There are job assignments available to inmates, based on a general record review of their case, sentence, medical history, general conduct, and previous work history if applicable. It is common practice to try and supply all inmates with a job who qualify to work whether they request it or not, but at the present time this is difficult due to the large numbers of people coming to jail and a shortage of positions available. Over time, there have been positions and programs that have been eliminated or placed on hold that provided job opportunities and educational benefits to inmates. This also has helped to create the shortage, and limit some of the rehabilitative opportunities previously open to inmates. It is interesting to note that whether an inmate submits a request to work or not - if they are assigned a job and refuse to work, they are subject to a misconduct. The system does attempt to prevent total idleness whenever possible.

There are many things available to people coming to jail that were not available to them on the street due to their lifestyles. Even an education can be acquired. At the present time, the system is attempting to make sure that anyone who does not have a high school diploma or GED and would like to get one, has the opportunity to do so. Some institutions, depending on location and proximity to a college, do offer the opportunity to earn an associates' degree in certain areas, or even a bachelor's degree. A certificate in business may also be obtained depending on the institution one may be housed at. I do know a couple of cases where inmates earned a masters degree while incarcerated, but this was accomplished by correspondence courses, and is not offered as a standard option throughout the jail system. This will be discussed in more detail in the chapter on rehabilitation.

A wise convict - someone with some wisdom - takes advantage of these opportunities and uses them to the fullest advantage. Some do think ahead and realize that they will re-enter society at some point, and they realize that they will need more to survive than what they came to jail with. Unfortunately, all too many people do not take advantage of these opportunities and make the best use of their time in jail, and return to the street just as illiterate, just as unskilled, and equally unfortunate as when they came. Unfortunately in todays frenzied world we live in, our needs, wants, and priorities are at times drastically out of proportion. Many times, they are dictated by pressures of society, economics, social status, and the desire to survive and be accepted. This brings us to another facet of inmate life. Acceptance.

One interesting observation as far as inmates, is the need for acceptance and individuality. By staff, by fellow inmates, by visitors, and by society. Everyone of course has the need to be accepted and be noticed as individuals, but it appears that this need is very much heightened in jail. We must remember that some of the dysfunctional lives that these men and women led on the street, have helped to create this tremendous need for acceptance and individuality. Things such as a certain pair of glasses, a unique hairstyle, or a certain brand or type of sneakers all help to create this distinction. Some inmates often will tell you anything you want to hear or offer constant compliments, so you will be more inclined to accept them and think good of them.

Most inmates will never admit to any guilt or involvement when it comes to the crime they were convicted of. People on the street often joke about the professed innocence claimed by inmates, making reference to statements like "I didn't do it", or "I wasn't there when it happened", or it wasn't my gun", or the ever popular phrase "it was a set-up". In some cases, one or any of these could be very true, but these statements have been made many times out of fear of rejection and being looked at as just another common criminal. Let's face it - it would be hard for many of us to admit we did some of the things that people in jail have been convicted of, and to the degree that they did them - without the fear of being an outcast by family, friends, and society. It is difficult at times for the convicted party to admit it to themselves, let alone confess it to a stranger who might have no sympathy or understanding towards them or their circumstances - especially if they are indeed guilty.

Nevertheless, there are those who speak with a smooth tongue, and wear the outfit of con-man as if tailor made. Some of the most suave and debonair people you could ever hope to meet exist in jails.

There are those who will do unbelievable and unexpected favors, in the all - out attempt for acceptance. The pureness of their motives usually remains to be seen. Unfortunately on the street, some went so far as to kill someone for the same purpose. They really did not want to kill them, but to save face and reputation among their peers, they followed through with it. Gang war killings, very common in the 60's and 70's, are a perfect example. Many of these individuals later live to regret the act they performed in the name of acceptance or reputation. I know men here who have given the system 25 years or more for such a name. The same men, if they are totally honest, will admit to you what a senseless act it was, and how much they wish they could turn back the hands of time.

One of the main factors contributing to this need to be known and noticed is the condition of incarceration itself. One thing people do not realize is that when a person enters the jail system, they are literally stripped of everything. Their clothes are taken, even if they are already in prison garb from another jail, and new prison clothes are issued. All personal belongings with the exception of earrings, watches, a wedding ring, or a chain which occasionally dangles a religious medal, are confiscated and locked up or sent home. The individual is issued an admission pack containing a toothbrush, toothpaste, shaving cream, razor, drinking cup, comb, and two blank mailing envelopes. I laugh sometimes when I think of the envelopes being issued without paper or objects to write with. Since I see the inmates the following morning after they arrive, it is not uncommon to be asked if I could spare some paper or a pencil to write a letter.

As for old things being taken and new things being issued, a new identification is first and foremost. The inmate receives his or her number, by which they are known and referred to mostly everywhere they are throughout the jail and the entire system. Basically, the individual takes on a new identity when entering prison. He or she is now a number, dressed like everyone else, eating the same food as everyone else, even down to getting locked into their house the same time as everyone else. Inmates are basically locked in their cells for the night around 9:00 p.m. and remain there until about 6:00 a.m. the following morning. Exceptions to this are the ones who are working, have a medical emergency, or of course, are locked in the Restricted Housing Unit for one reason or another, which is basically 23 hour a day lock-up with 1 hour out for exercise if they choose to take advantage of it. Imagine living on a street where everyone is in the house by 9:00 p.m.!

It sometimes makes me laugh when I hear the men who return on a parole violation for violating their curfew times. I'll ask them why they violated, and they will usually say things like "there's no way I'm gonna be in by 9:00 pm on the street man - what do they think I am, a kid or something?" To which I usually reply "Hey, what time do you have to be in now?" Of course much to their embarrassment, they usually see the absurdity in their statement whether they will admit it or not. They quickly see that their reasoning was not the best. Obviously, it was better to have freedom and be in by a certain time, rather than to be confined and still be told to be in by a certain time. It all boils down to being responsible and taking responsibility for your life and actions. A secondary factor in this type of situation is the values placement concerning freedom versus confinement. Unfortunately, the latter is too often the case, and a lack of responsibility and value of freedom is often indicated.

This takes us to another subject concerning actions of inmates - - and probably the most outstanding reason for jails thriving and filling up so fast. Responsibility. Not taking responsibility. One of the leading reasons for the mammoth influx of people into the correctional system. Let's look at this in some greater depth in an attempt to tie together the facts concerning crime and recidivism.

First and foremost, we have established that inmates are human beings just like civilians. They have the same thoughts, same emotions, same desires, and same needs. In the inmate population, you have all extremes of individuals as far as race, religion, culture, I.Q., talent, and creativity. Inmates cry at night just like civilians do when faced with certain problems felt to be out of their control. Inmates have identical medical problems to civilians. Beyond that, they seek medical treatment just as people do on the outside, but within the confines of the system. Inmates get a designated number of visits per month (usually one for each Sunday of the month, and any days they choose by people of their choice and approval of the officials of the institution in which they are housed.) These visits are usually from family, friends, and legal counselors. Hygienic, cultural, spiritual, and health needs are met by a myriad of people such as barbers (of which are inmates), dentists, (who are not inmates), doctors (which some inmates think they are), nurses (which some inmates would like to get to know better), pastors, spiritual counselors, social workers and the like. In all honestly, the system does try very hard to meet all the needs of the person just as if they were in civilian life, some more successfully than others. So what is the difference between freedom and incarceration? Most will tell you the confinement and the limitations due to confinement.

Back to responsibility. Now, let me pose a question to you, the reader. If you, assuming you are a contributing member of society as far as taxes, family life, and community involvement, were offered the same things you now enjoy, with the exception of freedom to move about sometimes as you like: would it make a difference to you if you were told you had to be in your house at a certain time, and could only travel within a certain area, as long as you basically didn't have to change your lifestyle? This is a question only each reader could answer for themselves. If the answer is no, it would not make any difference, and you could adapt to the limits placed on you, then why would you bother to be a responsible person and attempt to do anything it takes to stay totally free? If it was no big deal either way, why bother to take the responsibility of following the law to the letter if it's easier the other way? Is the picture beginning to come together?

Because of this very example, many people say that jail is too easy, too soft, and too adaptable for the majority of inmates. They say that conditions and rules should be tougher with less privileges, so people would dread, or even fear coming back, and would do what ever it takes to stay out. I guess sort of like the bread and water days, with 23 hour a day lockup and one hour of exercise, a Bible in your cell, and very little contact with the outside world. Unfortunately, this dark-sided theory of corrections has never been proven to deter crime either.

Responsibility. What each of us must take from the time we can be held accountable for our actions, no matter how young. Unfortunately, I've met inmates that display less responsibility than my eight year old son. These individuals have no clue as to what the word means. Responsibility includes not only being accountable for your actions, but being able to look at consequences. The majority of men and women in jail did not look ahead to the consequences of their actions, they only acted -- or re-acted in some cases. Basically, no thought was given to the after effects of their actions. Cause and effect. Action and reaction. We all too often forget that the decisions we make today can and will effect the rest of our lives in both positive and negative ways.

The individual who put the gun on and went to the corner store to take some money or merchandise to feed his drug habit -- or his family, which ever the case - might not have really counted on shooting the person behind the counter, but hopefully just intimidating them - - but it happened. A quick move, a refusal to give up the money or goods, a physical fight - - whatever the situation. The last thing the taker wanted was a body. Now, after the fact, was the money or merchandise worth a life sentence or the death penalty? I can tell you this - - not even ten Brinks trucks full of $500.00 bills is worth the rest of your life behind bars or being executed, much less the few dollars that were in that cash register, or the victim's pocket, or the little bit of merchandise that could be carried out while fleeing the scene.

One very important ingredient was missing here in this persons character, or lack of it. Responsibility. Taking responsibility for his life and actions. It's too late to cry about your actions once you've acted. Or, as they say, you can't call the bullet back. If the man in the situation had taken the responsibility of getting an education to better be able to feed his family, or had gotten help for his drug habit or whatever the habit might be, this whole scenario might not have occurred. Unfortunately, there are hundreds of thousands of individuals who fit right into this picture like a glove, some with different situations of course, but the same end result. A life of incarceration due to a lack of responsibility.

In all fairness to victim and perpetrator, and for the purpose of general information, we must remember that responsibility does not just happen. It is a learned and acquired trait that is taught from a very young age. Parents are to be the sole teachers, and by example, are very influential. Likewise, if the display is not there along with the absence of verbiage, the trait will be greatly lacking. This is all too often the case in our society when economics, self-fulfillment and desperation tend to quash proper parenting.

In a great number of inmates, responsibility is, for the most part, largely lacking or almost non-existent. Lists of excuses and justifications are a mile long as to why they committed the crime or violation. The ones I've heard are too numerous to count. Everything from personality conflicts to down and out simple survival needs. In the wide gap between, there are things like drug and alcohol addiction that lead to the crime, domestic disputes, the desire for more and more money or power, and just the plain thrill of committing a certain act or crime.

There is only one problem with these situations. No judge or jury tends to look favorably on crime. The more aggravating the circumstances, the more impact it may have on anyone hearing the case. Even though some courts may tend to show more leniency than others, the criminal at that point - - or should we say the defendant - - is still at the mercy of the court. Sort of like the victim being at the mercy of the perpetrator. Isn't it amazing how situations can turn around and sneak up to haunt us. But once again, most people committing crimes do not take even a second to study the consequences, much less want to take responsibility for their actions after the fact.

In all fairness, I would like to comment on people, namely men, who return to prison on domestic related charges. This area provides many pitfalls for men on parole, and accounts for a good number of men coming back to jail. With angry words, verbal threats, or even stale relationships, the possibility of returning to jail grows even stronger. All it takes in many cases is a phone call from the woman of the house, or some woman in their life, and the trip back to prison is short and swift. I have often said, that the parole system is a very dangerous tool in the hands of a woman, who for almost any reason (including a new partner, spouse, lover, or whatever) wants to see the man out of their life. It is one thing to blow the whistle on a man who is threatening and/or physically violent, but it is quite another to use the system as a sort of "scandalous scalpel" - cutting the unwanted party out of the picture to make way for the "new interest" at hand.

I would like to say at this point that most inmates, everything considered, are just like anyone on a daily basis in free society. I have found this to be true with everyone from credit card or food stamp scammers to serial killers. Even those deemed the most dangerous criminals throughout the state in all or any respects (of which Graterford houses many) are usually cordial and cooperative when being dealt with in the medical realm.

Since my dealings with inmates centers around medical diagnosis and care, I certainly do not see all aspects of the inmates' character during the course of a day as would the correctional officers who are with the inmates all the time. But, if I were to just believe the media hype and prison stories that I've heard in the past, and not have actually worked in the prison environment, I certainly could not make the same evaluation. Movies and stories have made all these incarcerated individuals seem like dregs of society who are writhing animals just looking to prey on innocent people. Most stories I've heard about inmates fit this description. Even some employees working within the system, who tend to allow their prejudices to surface at times, will speak very negatively about inmates.

Contrary to popular belief, this is far from the truth. True enough, there are seemingly incorrigible inmates here that most of us would not want living in our neighborhoods. There are those who are rude, arrogant, rebellious, and outright nasty. There are those who display aberrant behavior and violent actions - assaulting staff members and other inmates seemingly every chance they get. Some of these individuals appear to be very slow learners; knowing and physically feeling the consequences of their actions, but continuing to do the same things over and over again to warrant disciplinary action. It should be understood that the capacity in which one functions as an employee within the system, certainly may effect the view of inmates from their standpoint, depending on the closeness or distance to the inmates in which they work with. But, on the whole, I have found that most inmates are very decent people to deal with.

Personally, in dealing with inmates, I always maintained the position that I was neither Judge nor jury for them, nor was I hired to make them suffer at all for the crimes they were convicted of. Suffering comes easily enough just by virtue of conviction and incarceration, without employees feeling the personal need to enhance or quicken it. Personal vendettas in jail usually only lead to one thing - more personal vendettas.

It is a fact, that some of the nicest and most intelligent people I've ever met were - - yes, incarcerated. Convicted of a crime and sentenced to do time. I've met and gotten to know men who, if you put them in a suit and give them a briefcase, you would think were C.E.O.'s of a corporation. Ironically, some were bankers, lawyers, physicists, contractors, architects, physicians, and the like. Professional people doing very unprofessional things - for unscrupulous and devious reasons. Remember, nice does not necessarily equate honesty, morality, integrity, or responibility - nor does it mean one is safe to be around - just for the record.

Make no mistake about it. There are also the ones who perfectly fit the role of T.V. killer, madman, gangster and so on. In a jail of this size with anywhere from 3,000 to 3,400 inmates, you have every extreme of every facet of life as I mentioned before. In prison, you have the best of the best. The best con-men, arsonists, schemers, deceivers, locksmiths, safecrackers, auto thieves, forgers, and triggermen. We house men who have killed for as little as $10.00 or a bottle of wine, on up to millions of dollars. We have a special needs area and mental health unit that houses people who committed very ghastly deeds - - brutal murder, decapitations, body dismemberment and the like. A few went so far as to consume and digest the body parts they dismembered. It seems very unfair and unorthodox to place check forgers and credit card scammers with people of extreme uncivilized crimes, but this is a common practice in the system. Don't forget, the prison is the prime educational setting for knowledge in all the criminal ways of life. What you do not know about crime and illegal practice when coming here, you can and will know if you so desire to, by the time you leave here - if you indeed leave. Nevertheless, it is a known fact that people of all behavioral extremes co-habitate here.

Usually, only if you are a known threat to yourself or to others are you confined to a specific area. Over the years I've seen a number of men who walk around in a sort of semi-hypnotic, semi-comatose state just surviving - - living on medication and being pointed in the right direction from day to day. It is interesting to note that some inmates feel sorry for some of these individuals, as they do for the elderly or disabled, and will look out for them on a daily basis. Not only for their physical protection, but also for their cosmetic, hygienic, and dietary needs. Some of the others are rejected for the most part.

I've often wondered why some are looked out for and others are not.

I've been told that it has to do with the type of case they have or their ability to deal with prison life. I've talked to inmates who feel the need to shelter someone unfortunate due to the fact that they themselves were never sheltered. Others feel it's the least they can do in connection with remorse they have concerning their particular crime against society. Then others simply feel sorry for the unfortunate and take it upon themselves to watch out for them. It's very interesting in the prison setting to see some of society's labeled "criminals and incorrigibles" take someone under their wing and treat them like a dear brother. It is on this level that you see the human side of inhumanity as society labels it, and the general theory of inmates goes right out the window. Just because a person gets caught up in unfortunate circumstances or reacts in the wrong way in a situation, does not mean they are a hardened criminal or uncaring human being. This has been proven many times over in the prison environment. Many inmates are street smart, with some possessing a fair degree of intelligence but often times fail or failed to use good judgement.

Working around and in close contact with inmates is nothing less than interesting. Their habits, ways of thinking and reasoning, rationale, and psychology are all things that need to be experienced personally to fully understand their nature. When asked the questions on the street like "what are those guys really like, aren't you afraid to work in there, etc., etc., etc., "- if I feel like playing into their anticipated answer, I might reply "Big, mean, and ugly!", in a loud, assertive voice, "tattoos muscles, and sweat - they're animals!" Then, after a short pause, and their anticipated response, I simply respond, "they are like you and I. And no, I'm not afraid to work there." If you are afraid to work in there you shouldn't be there. If hearing gates and doors slam behind you sends chills up your spine, it's the wrong place for you. If hearing chains and handcuffs rattling unnerves you, you're in the wrong field. There are certain people that just cannot work in the prison environment.

I often tell people who ask me this question, that I am much more apprehensive about sitting and eating in a fast food restaurant or going to a shopping mall than going into the prison everyday to work. The chances of getting shot or maimed in a jail are far less than if eating out or shopping somewhere. You can be relatively sure that you won't see any guns or weapons at close range, or at all for that matter, when working in a prison. Don't get me wrong, there are weapons in jails, usually in the form of homemade knives, but the chances of a civilian seeing them or coming in contact with them are very, very rare.

This was demonstrated to me one time years ago, after I was absolutely sure that the demonstrator had no weapon concealed. After a 360 degree turn and arms raised in the air, I would have bet my paycheck that there was no weapon concealed - or so I thought. There was absolutely nothing unusual about him that I saw, until he reached under his shirt in the back, and pulled out a shank (homemade knife), with a blade about 6 to 8 inches in length, one inch wide and sharpened on both edges, and about a 5 inch handle made of tightly wound electrical tape. Sharp as a razor and about 12 inches long overall, it removed all doubt about concealed weapons, and revealed to me yet another facet of real jail life. The weapons generally are concealed and hidden, used on other inmates, and rarely surface except in a search endeavor or incident. It was strange enough to see the weapon and hold it in the first place, but even stranger to think that these "tools of the trade" in many inmate conflicts were once pieces of a bed, chair, sink, machinery, or other objects around the jail. Deadly as they may be, their existence and locations are little known to most employees, and much more concealed and rarely surfacing than most guns and weapons on the street.

A strange concept when you really think about it. Safer behind bars with the assumed criminals than out in the free world with all the "normal people". Of course, that depends on your definition of normal. In fact, after working in an emergency room for many years, I can definitely testify to the fact that my life was threatened many more times than it ever was in jail, and by visible raging tempers and in some cases weapons to accompany them. Hatchets, guns, switchblades, bats

- to name a few. Highly excited, agitated, and volatile people, with only a little distance and air between you and them. Much more life threatening than anything the average prison employee ever experiences. In fact, I have never ever come close to any situation which was life threatening in all the years I've worked in the jail. I cannot make the same statement about my career in the hospital setting or even my visits to a shopping mall, where my son and I were caught once just feet from a very dangerous situation involving a psychopath on the rampage. By the way, I'm also a little leery about working in a Post Office. You never hear of a bank teller who was fired, coming back to the bank and killing all the tellers and supervisors - - or a dismissed department store clerk returning to kill all the clerks and bosses - - or even a nurse or hospital administrator let go due to budget cuts, returning to shoot the place up and kill everyone in their path. At least not yet. But I don't understand what it is about post offices. I'll take the prison any day over the mailroom.

Yes, some say there is a tremendous amount of stress in the postal office setting, but I can tell you this - - you haven't seen stress until you witness the prison environment, especially in a large prison such as Graterford. Without exaggeration, you can see it on the faces of some inmates and employees alike as if it were written there with a magic marker. It's in their voices, on their faces, and in their demeanor. As "too caring" as it might sound to most, considering some of the crimes committed by these inmates, the blunt of the stress is absorbed much of the time by the inmates rather than the civilians. There are many angry words exchanged on a daily basis, or minor altercations that occur due to stress carried into the prison by civilians. It is not really an issue of right or wrong, but more just a usual occurrence of human nature. Many people today are having a very difficult time dealing with the common pressures of life and survival. There are situations occurring daily in households and relationships that seem unmanageable and of course carry right over into the job place. These seemingly unmanageable stresses and pressures carried into the occupational world that most of us are in eight hours a day, five days a week on the average, contribute to a melting pot of potential volatile situations.

In the prison setting as it is, you already have volatile individuals due to circumstances beyond their immediate control, trying to relieve stress, not enhance it. Incarceration itself tends to produce very high stress levels due to the environment. When civilians report to work bound up with stress, inmates tend to be the targets of release along with co-workers occasionally. I've seen many civilians hurt due to a careless word or over-reaction said in a threatening tone. Don't be deceived - there are inmates working around you being seemingly nice people, even to the point of being courteous and helpful, that are loaded guns with the trigger cocked so to say. A mean word, an angry look or mistaken gesture could and has caused the hammer to fall. The inmate explodes in a moment of rage, hurting or killing the individual, with the potential of inciting other volatile inmates to join in. This is not an uncommon occurrence in jails, and has sparked the formation of stress release programs for prison workers nationwide. Many jails also have organized stress release programs for inmates in an attempt to quell some of these potentially dangerous situations. It has been proven time and time again that if one or the other parties involved in one of those scenarios would have just walked away or known when to shut up as things escalated, the situation could have been defused very easily. Unfortunately, the combination of stress and ego sometimes tend to dull our common sense. The end result is often more unfortunate for the civilian than the inmate.

So what do inmates do to release stress? How do they vent their anger and frustration? There are many avenues of stress release in jail. One of the most popular ways is going to the weight pile and pumping iron. This is one representation of jailhouse T.V. that is very accurate. When you see the guys pumping iron at the weight pile with all the tattoos, bulging biceps and pecs', be assured that it is accurate. Some of the largest people I have ever seen are in prison. There are men who come here at 135 lbs. with negative muscle mass, and now are 215 lbs. of solid serious muscle. Even the ones that are not really that bulky and without much definition are relatively strong. I remember going to a weightlifting competition and noticing a rather thin, non-developed guy on a team from another jail. Basically, when you looked around, you saw guys who fit the image of power lifters and weight lifters. This person seemed to be out of place. Much to my surprise, he laid down on the bench and pressed 210 pounds!

Another individual that sticks in my mind, among many, is a guy who worked up in our infirmary area as a janitor. He was a lifer, convicted of first degree murder. During this time in jail, even though he was an athlete prior to coming to jail, he discovered some hidden potential. He seemed to be particularly good at squats, among other areas of weight lifting. His stature was perfect for that division of weight lifting, being about 5'6" tall and weighing about 245 lbs. He was built like a human fire hydrant. Short, stocky, strong, and not a great distance to go from the floor to a standing position. His last unofficial squat record, which by the way I have a signed picture of him performing, recorded at 1,010 lbs. Normally in competition, he would easily do 925 lbs., to 950 lbs. or so officially. The last I had heard, he held both official and unofficial United States and World records for his weight class. There are many men that have come to jail and found hidden potential and talent in weight lifting. It is one of the best releases of stress, among other sports, that exists in the system.

Physical exercise and sports seem to be very popular for stress release in jail, and inmates take it very seriously. As one inmate once said, "we take sports and exercise as serious as the parole board." Some enjoy the camaraderie of team sports, while others lean toward individual competition and accomplishment. I've known many men who love to do calisthenics rather than go the weight pile or the gym. I'll never forget a guy I talked to one day who was complaining of shoulder pain. I questioned him as to the possible reason for the pain. He proceeded to tell me that there was no injury that he remembered, but that he does exercise a lot. I asked him what "a lot" meant, and what type of exercise it was. He told me he basically does push-ups and crunches. Looking at his stature, something told me to ask him some numbers out of curiosity. His present workout consisted of 1300 push-ups daily, done in sets of 50 until reaching 1300 - - non stop, with one minute rest in between sets. My shoulders began to ache just thinking about it! As for the crunches, 300 consecutively was the daily number. The stress of doing all those alone would be too much for most people. It is interesting to note however, that most of the big weight lifters are actually big teddy bears!

In reality, some of the most aggressive, toughest guys I know, who are quick with their hands and can fight, are some of the smallest. Naturally you have average and large sized men who are good fighters, but contrary to T.V. jail, the big huge guys are not necessarily the tough guys. I learned that very early in my career here. As a guy said to me once concerning this subject - - "Remember, big and strong, yes. Quick and agile, rarely. It is rare to find a large, super strength individual with hands of lighting to match. The real big guys just don't have the speed, and the small guys don't have quite the strength, but somehow it balances out." As I mentioned before, you find all extremes in jail.

Other stress releases include boxing, basketball, baseball, football, music, art, and educational programs. Again, and most unfortunately, some of these individuals never realized their hidden potential, or at least never developed it, until coming to jail. In fact, as far as art work, some of the most creative and undoubtedly the most beautiful drawings and paintings I've ever seen were done right here in jail. Given the proper tools, and placed in a cell with nothing but time on your hands, you can become very creative. One individual that comes to my mind, who now unfortunately is deceased, is a man that I knew for many years here. His work will be remembered for a long time by inmates and civilians alike. His specialty was wildlife and landscapes. Many of the animals appeared to almost jump right off the canvas at you due to looking so life - like. At least one of his works were always chosen for the yearly calendar put out by the D.O.C., that would hang in offices and areas throughout every jail in the State of Pennsylvania, among other facilities. He was surely an individual who could have made a nice living using his talent to paint and draw, and perhaps have owned his own studio or gallery; but a combination of bad childhood circumstances and bad decisions eventually led him down a different road. Remember, the decisions we make every minute of every day can and will undoubtedly affect the rest of our lives. Jails are full, and continuously filling up more, with people who are the products of bad decisions.

The jail setting overall, at least as far as an all male prison is concerned, is a complex mix of some of the most masculine, masterminding, manipulative, and in some cases mild mannered individuals placed in an environment, ever filled with rage, anger, hostility, vengeance, and hopelessness. Every extreme in lifestyles, both passive and aggressive, varying from straight laced conservative to far deviate in varied preferences, exists in prison. Normal in many cases is anything the individual wants it to be, so as to justify their actions and standards. All extremes exist here, and that includes inmates and civilians alike. Many fearful of rats, bats, and roaches, but not shackles and shotguns (or knives and handguns if you prefer). Exteriorly tough, but many interiorly tender. A society of people who for the most part calloused themselves to the ways of God and the ways of society as a whole. For the most part opportunists, but lacking optimism. Many with a dim outlook, growing dimmer the more they look out. Their only hope for the future is that they hope they have a future. An unnatural environment filled with people seeking the natural. Seeking to meet that need and fill that void that is ever present in the world of incarceration.

Ultimately, trying to go home - - or at least be free. Spiritual freedom, of course, is the ultimate freedom. For where physical freedom may end and does end at some point, spiritual freedom continues. Physically bound, but yet free. You can bind a man's arms and legs to a point of total immobilization, but you can never restrain or confine, what is in his heart and mind. To be at peace with God and know his saving grace, mercy, and compassion on a personal level is what every prison inhabitant wants and needs, whether they know it or not. The true freedom that every incarcerated individual really needs is not limited to the reduction of physical restraints, but rather the induction of God's ways into the soul of man, so as to fulfill His plan for our lives while here on earth. Then and only then, can prison inhabitants truly be set free.

Speaking of Inmates

One of the satisfactions I get from working in the prison and having close contact with inmates (though many feel no satisfaction working in a jail) is undoubtedly the hearing and seeing of stories, terms and varied mannerisms of the inmates. They in many cases, do not try to be funny and amusing, but rather come across that way naturally. In case you didn't know, there is a definite difference between the mannerisms and rhetoric associated with a country person as opposed to one from the inner city. Growing up on a farm in the country, I could talk at length about planting crops, harvesting, farm equipment, farm animals, and we usually called each other by our birthright names. Not so with people from the "big city". A different way of referring to people, and totally different conversation. That's what makes all of us so unique - different names, speech, dress, and mannerisms.

Being the closest State prison to Philadelphia, and again the largest in the State, naturally we receive most of our inmates from the city itself. With the majority of receptions being Black, plus a fair number of Hispanics mixed in, the white Caucasian population of the jail no longer forms the majority. This factor does open the door to a different type of humor and mannerisms that are typical to a predominately "White" jail or White crowd so to say. Having grown up in a neighborhood with only four Black families, (two of which you never saw come out of the house) and having attended a high school of over 1500 students, with about 10 or 20 Blacks and two Hispanics - coming to work in a prison as a minority was nothing short of enlightening!

Expressions such a "homie", or homies" (meaning you are from the same neighborhood) "rappie" or "rap partner", (someone involved in the same case as yours), "road dog", "roadie", or walkie" (your best buddy or partner) just to name a few, are commonly heard throughout everyday conversation. These accompanying some mentioned earlier pertaining to an inmate's cell, tend to give the verbiage a little "color", if you will excuse the expression. When addressing one another, it is very common to hear shortened names or nicknames used on a regular basis. Even age commands certain terminology, like "old head" for older man, and "young buck" for a much younger man in age. One has not heard nicknames until experiencing an environment with about 2,800 inner city Black males, all conversing on the same level about the same things in general, and many being from the same neighborhood from little on up!

Very interesting nicknames to say the least, and their origin none the less interesting. Boxers for instance, might adopt a name carrying a connotation of hitting hard, knocking out, or "putting one to sleep". "Ice", "slam", "knockout", "champ", "dust em", just to name a few. Then there are those who adopt names of animals for one reason or another, carrying good or bad references with them. "Dog", "cat", "puma", "cheetah", "bird", "snake", or "rat" just to name a few. Some are given names by peers that tend to reflect something they do or used on a regular basis, or that might have happened during the course of a crime, a type of car they are used to driving, or just reflect a certain mannerism or characteristic they have. I've heard names such as "bum", "cool", "wine", "dutch", "slick", "money", "top cat", (a popular cartoon character many years ago), "country", "saint", "reaper", "bop", "12 guage", "cadillac", "4 wheel", "top gun", "pop corn", and a host of others too numerous to mention. One of the more notable ones I remember hearing was "graveyard", so nicknamed because he allegedly jumped in the back of a hearse during a funeral procession while being chased by the police. Some way to elude the police!

At the same time, some inmates choose to use an alias that they were arrested under, which at times causes confusion when trying to match up old records. This among other reasons is precisely why inmates are tracked by numbers and not name only.

Others, solely for religious purposes, choose to be addressed by names with meaning and purpose associated with their faith and beliefs. This most commonly is seen in the Islamic Community where some choose to legally change their birthright name to an Islamic one. Many just adopt an Islamic name in addition to their birthright name, and use their new name as their identification along with their inmate number. Islamic names are chosen, or should we say are supposed to be chosen according to the religion, as a basis of personal characterization and attributes. Usually these names are chosen as a first, middle, and last name, just as anyone else would be given a first, middle, and last name at birth. Some very commonly heard are Rakeem, Saleem, Rasheed, Ali, Malik, Abdullah, Muhammad, and Yusuf, among others.

So, you might ask "what's in a name"? In the jail environment, a name can and does mean a whole lot.

As plentiful and colorful as all the names and nicknames around the jail, so are the stories that circulate pertaining to inmates and their everyday lives, both past and present. I would venture to say that for every one story I hear and remember for any length of time, there are probably ten or fifteen that I hear and quickly forget. Other than the few written in other parts of the book, there are some I took the time to write down, either while they were occurring or shortly after. Names were changed of course to protect identities, and accuracy is only as good as the one presenting the facts. Hopefully you will find them somewhat amusing, as I did. (Try to imagine yourself in the inmates situation, realizing the limitations and complications of being locked up.)

Being the first civilian X-ray technologist ever to work at Graterford, I was greeted with many different responses by inmates. Prior to my working there, inmates in those days worked in many capacities throughout the infirmary area. Inmates took the X-rays, drew the blood in the lab, worked as dental assistants, medical records clerks, sick call clerks, operating room assistants, and performed various nursing duties assisting in baths, bedpan changes, blood pressures, temps, and of course janitorial duties. Inmates were the bulk of the work force in the infirmary area, with nurses and supervisors overseeing the operation and performing the more skilled and supervisory duties.

When I arrived, inmates quickly formed varying opinions on me having taken the position that was one of the most valued jobs throughout the jail for inmates. Not only was it a great position in which to learn a profession while incarcerated, it was also in a nice quiet area away from the majority of the noise and confusion in the jail. It was also one of the highest paying jobs that an inmate could have throughout the institution. Nevertheless, it would definitely prove to be a trial by fire for me.

As the word began to spread that an "outsider" was now taking the X-rays, I encountered many different reactions as days and weeks went on. Inmates would now analyze this newcomer that was now replacing a fellow inmate. Fortunately for me, the inmate that was doing the radiology work before my arrival remained as an assistant, and in many cases helped to soften the blow throughout the inmate population. Being well known and well respected by many staff and inmates throughout the entire jail, his influence helped to convince many that the situation was not too bad after all. Three other inmates who were well known to many throughout the jail and previously did the X-ray work, also helped to ease fears and suspicions as time went on, as they now worked in other jobs around the jail. The D.O.C. at this point in time was merely trying to implement more professionalism throughout its' medical facilities by way of certification, licensures, and credentials. Also at this time in history, litigation was becoming more prevalent, and trained, licensed, and certified allied health care individuals were needed to upgrade standards throughout the jail system. Inmates were beginning to sue other inmates along with the Commonwealth due to accidents and mistakes made by untrained or registered personnel. Patient confidentiality was also becoming more of an issue, due to the fact that inmates were working with medical records, and had access to personal information. Consequently, the D.O.C. had to change and upgrade its' standards, and limit or eliminate certain jobs being performed by inmates, on or for other inmates. This did not say that the inmates were not doing a good job, and in fact they were - but, it revealed changing times in the D.O.C. operations, and the prison health care delivery system would not be exempt from those changes.

This created the need for employment of trained, certified civilians in the areas of Radiology, Lab, Dental, Nursing and

Medical Records. So began the phasing out of all inmates working in the infirmary area for anything other than janitorial duties, which of course we still depend on heavily today. Inmates played and still do play a vital part in the cleanliness and maintenance of the physical aspect of the infirmary area, as in most areas of the jail, and the disposal of the trash and waste generated daily.

In the days, weeks, months, and even a year or two after this transition, I encountered some interesting comments and reactions as I previously mentioned, in this position that I "stole from the inmates", as one inmate referred to it. I was greeted daily with everything from warm hellos to candid, callous "who are you's?"

I can recall one time when a certain inmate entered the room, fixed a gaze on me that would penetrate steel, and then cordially said hello to the inmate working with me. They happened to be long time friends, so I was introduced to this large, seemingly mad at the world individual as he appeared with no expression. As I shook his unwilling hand, he fixed his callous gaze on me that I have never forgotten, and simply said "you the one who took his job?" referring to my inmate assistant. No hi, hello, or nice to meet you. Nothing except that comment. I felt fortunate at that moment that there was one other person in the room who was on my side - at least occupationally speaking - and he quickly reassured his inmate friend that I didn't really take his job, but was there in addition to it. A civilian supervisor for the most part. Little did any of us know, that within a year or so from then, I would indeed be taking his job, and he would be there only as a janitor, and no longer taking any X-rays.

If first impressions mean anything, and stereotypes are at all accurate, this guy at that moment certainly fit my idea and definition of the big, mean black guy who you do not want to be caught in an alley with at night - or for the most part, my perception of the average prison inmate. Of course, that was coming from a little white guy's perspective, who watched prison movies on T.V. As I established a rapport with this individual through the years (which was tough because he never talked much anyway), I was able to see through the first impression phase of his callous demeanor, and we did get along rather well.

There were many other reactions similar to his, though probably not as extreme, and some I'm convinced were purely out of racial difference. In a predominately black male prison setting, a civilian Caucasian male coming in to take a black inmates job away, or deprive them of one more opportunity as some viewed it, just was hard to swallow. I fully understood this, and worked diligently to reverse that mindset. As I said earlier, it was trial by fire and a test of time. Every ounce of respect and trust had to be earned. And, as I quickly found out, inmates are very perceptive and know whether you are for real or not. It's both a learned and instinctive trait that helps one to survive as an inmate.

It was interesting that some were very open to the new change, regardless of race or color, and welcomed the outside professional with open arms. Some were leery at first, refusing to have certain studies done if an inmate would not be doing them. Others were relieved that a fellow inmate would now not be performing their diagnostic and healthcare needs any more, or have access to their personal medical files. As time went on, and more and more inmates got used to the total civilian health care setting, the apprehension grew less and less, and more and more inmates began taking advantage of the services being offered. I think it is funny now to watch people's expressions who knew nothing about those days - whether it be civilian or inmate, when you mention the fact that inmates drew blood, took X-rays, did nursing care, assisted the dentist and surgeon, and filed medical records. Their mouths drop open, their eyes get big, and they adopt a sudden look of disbelief. To coin a modern phrase and as hard as it is to image, the inmates were "all that" in those days.

I did come to learn that many inmates at times tend to view changes like this as just one more step in removing privileges or limiting ways of improvement and opportunity, and may fail to see the positive side and better end result. Back in those days and prior, many inmates only trusted other inmates due to bad things that happened in jails that were usually dismissed as "accidents". Some feel that way even today. Not even considering any racial or religious barriers, the mere fact that you were not an inmate was reason enough to be leery of your intentions. This is very understandable in a world where one has basically no control over their environment, is always being told "no" to things needed or desired, and what few possessions one may acquire are limited and sometimes confiscated.

Nevertheless, I can vividly recall one of my first few days as I'm going about my job seeing one patient after the next for X-rays. I took notice that most were relatively pleasant despite their circumstances. Hard to comprehend at first, imagining how I would feel being locked up away from family and society. As inmates entered and left, many would greet me with "hi, how you feelin" or "hey, what's up?" Upon leaving, many would offer a "thanks", "thanks man", "thanks man, take care", or "have a good day" (or "nice day"). If it was before a holiday, many would wish me and my family a great holiday. I found myself returning the wish or greeting as it was given to me out of cordiality, until I stopped to think about it for a moment. I thought to myself "my God, what am I saying?" "I'm probably hurting everyone of these guys feelings by telling them that stuff." I later learned that most inmates understand and appreciate those comments, fully realizing the cordiality intended, regardless of their situation. I also learned in time that most inmates will learn to make the best of a bad situation. Regardless, one of the most awkward things for me to say to an inmate, even after all these years of close contact, is "have a nice holiday", or "have a good day", or return their wish to me by saying "same to you". I guess its just a personal thing with me, wishing someone a good day or a nice holiday in such a terrible environment, but maybe it offers a note of encouragement in spite of it all. I certainly hope so.

Not only do inmates know how to make the best of a bad situation, but they also make some of the most unique things one ever saw out of items that most of us discard as trash or junk. I learned this one day as I was throwing away some white cardboard that comes in packs of X-ray film and is used solely for rigidity in each pack. I also was throwing out some plastic cups and lids that a substance called Barium comes in, and is used in radiology for studies of the gastrointestinal system. An inmate happened to be close by and "peeped" this (jail slang for "saw it"), and yelled to me to "hold up" (wait a minute, again in jail slang). He asked me why I was throwing away that good stuff - to which I looked around for any "good stuff" in the area. I said "you mean this trash?"

He rushed over as if there was a one hundred dollar bill laying there. With a smile on his face as if he had just discovered buried treasure, he said "you know what I could do with this?" to which I replied, "no, what?"

He began gathering up the cardboard and cups, and politely told me that you do not throw anything away in jail. He pointed out to me that most things one throws away on the street can and do become very useful in the very limited environment of jail. He showed me how those plastic cups quickly become "jailhouse tupperware" for food and beverages, and the white cardboard is very useful for jailhouse greeting cards, signs, and posters.

Some of the nicest and most unique cards and posters complete with dried flowers (also found in the trash or are given before discarding) have been produced with this "trash".

I believe the state system could greatly benefit from practicing some recycling and resourcefulness such as is common among convicts.

Speaking of things being taken that vary in value to us, just a short time ago I had a guy walk in my room, we exchanged some friendly conversation, but I noticed his eyes darting around the room as if to notice or memorize everything he saw. Passing it off as general curiosity, I walked into the next room to make his I.D. for the X-ray, then walked back out. Routinely, I have a piece of tape that I use to tape the I.D. to the film, and between uses it hangs on the wall where he stood. It happened to not be there, so I retraced my steps, only to find it still missing. The tape I can get more of, but the left marker attached to it is vital. I stopped, thought a minute, and looked again. I was just ready to end the search and improvise, when my eyes caught a piece of tape - covering the inmates belt buckle!

As a rule, you never put your hands on an inmate except to

help them or break up a fight. Something inside me rose up like a lion, and I reached out and grabbed the tape while stating "give me that tape!" My left marker still attached, I took it and placed it on the I.D. and continued to stare into his eyes. He was as surprised as I was aggressive, and stuttering and hesitating at the same time he said "but I need it - I need it for something." I looked at him, with what must have been a look of fury, and said loudly "why did you have to steal it?" He continued to appear surprised, bordering on dumbfounded, as I instantly hit him with "no wonder you're in jail!" Not another word left his mouth except a humble "thank you" when he walked out. I closed the door and thought about the whole scenario for a moment. This was a rare reaction on my part. Knowing that a reaction like that can get you hurt or killed in a jail, I questioned my reaction repeatedly in my mind. Was the stress getting to me? Was I in burnout? Was it just the principle of the thing? Probably a combination of all three, but certainly not worth my health or my life. It's amazing how much even a piece of tape is worth to someone.

Speaking of stealing, I talked to a guy one time who had come back on a parole violation which he thought was very unfair. He explained to me that he simply went down to the convenience store to buy a bottle of tylenol. He stated that he was waiting in line to pay for it and the clerk walked away. He said he got tired of waiting, and finally just walked out with the tylenol. Most convenience stores have cameras, so identifying is usually not a problem. After being arrested, he also was tested and came up with a hot urine, indicating the presence of a controlled substance. He felt it very unfair to be charged for theft and a parole violation for a simple bottle of tylenol, since he fully intended to pay for it anyway, but he just got tired of waiting. As he said, he did not mean to steal it, but the clerk didn't return soon enough! Interesting justification.

As justification goes, we all tend to try and justify things we did or would like to do, somehow. Among inmates, one may hear many justifications as far as actions and reactions they made. This does not say the judge, or jury, or parole board agrees with them, and most of the time they do not.

I recorded two stories, the first of which brought a man back to jail on a parole violation for getting married, but not telling his parole man. I tried to explain to him that his action was a definite wrong decision, due to the fact that usually it is a must that you notify the agent of any change in status which would include getting married. He proceeded to try and convince me of how much he and his girlfriend loved each other, and wanted to do the right thing by getting married. The only little glitch was that he was afraid if he told his parole agent, his intent might be frowned upon due to certain circumstances (which he did not care to go into). Obviously, if he had this fear or hesitation, the "circumstances" probably were not conducive to a good marriage or influence on the part of one or both people. According to the parole board, a violation such as this might tend to carry 3 to 6 months back in jail, and then re-parole, even though it is rare to return a person to jail at this point in time just for not reporting that they were married. Unfortunately, by skirting the parole officer and the rules set forth, now the man in this case has yet another "circumstance" to deal with.

The other story is no less amusing and certainly not unique. As mentioned before, some inmates on parole tend to try and bend the rules a little and attempt to justify actions as they feel necessary. Unfortunately, the parole board does not always accept this justification and reasoning of the parolee. The man in this situation had a drinking problem which helped to bring him to jail in the first place. When he left on parole, one of the strong stipulations was that he does not drink, among other things. He informed me as a new recent parole violator, that he felt it was very unfair that he came back to jail. He stated that he had done nothing wrong, and that he was just sitting in his house minding his own business when the parole officer knocked on the door. He said he politely got up from the football game he was watching and answered the door, inviting the parole officer in to sit down.

He told me the next thing he knew, he was being brought back to jail for a violation - drinking. He could not understand this, because he said he had not hurt anyone, and was home minding his own business, watching the game and having a beer!

Seeing that he was open for discussion, I stopped him immediately and asked him if he said he was drinking a beer. He said "sure, but I was in my own house minding my own business." I tried to explain to him, that regardless of where he was, or the fact that he was innocent of any crime, he was indeed drinking, and right in plain view of the parole officer. I told him the rules are the rules - for him, no alcohol, no time, no where, for no reason. He left my room still feeling very violated, and I think very discouraged because I did not sympathize with him more and agree with his justification. As he turned to what I imagined would be to say good-bye or thank me, he simply said "oh well. I don't understand it, that's the way it goes."

I've yet to figure out what part of "No" he didn't understand. Stories involving inmates that left on parole and returned are usually sort of amusing, not to the inmate of course, but to us who hear them everyday. They unfortunately tend to show the inability to assume responsibility, and take charge of certain problem areas in their lives that continue to bring them back to jail. Certain simple responsibilities that most of society has mastered such as punctuality, notification to supervision, being law abiding, or just being able to make good sound decisions, are not outstanding qualities associated with many parolees. In short, old habits and ways die hard.

This reminds me of a story about a man I got to know fairly well over the years who was a lifer and received a commutation, allowing him to go home on life parole status. He was always very quiet and conducted himself in a fashion fitting with the term "model prisoner". I can recall the day he told me that he received the commutation, and as tears began to well up in his eyes, he said simply, "I'm going home, after 22 years here, I'm going home."

Not too long after that, I had heard that he went home on his first furlow. For the first time in over 22 years, he went home to briefly enjoy all the pleasures most people have access to everyday in free society. The funny part was, he forgot how to enjoy them! He spoke of the car ride home, as if it were his first ride in a jumbo jet. He could not believe he could get out of the car, unescorted, with hands free of handcuffs. He was used to

101

this of course, but always on prison property, since he lived and worked in the outside service unit before going home. But, to actually do it 35 miles from the prison was a totally different realization.

Once in the house, his wife told him to get comfortable and re-acquaint himself with the surroundings. He remarked as to how nice it was to walk from room to room and not see one inmate! Pictures, wall hangings, decorations, furniture, all bringing back memories of times past. He said at one point he was sitting in the living room, and asked his wife if he could have something to eat. She said of course, it's your house too! He found himself apologizing, and informed her that for 22 years he could only eat at certain times of the day, other than food he stored in his cell or footlocker, and he never had the option of just walking to the refrigerator and taking what he wanted. She understood.

A little later, he inquired about a shower. She laughed, and showed him the towels and soap. He felt foolish, but for the last 22 plus years, he could only shower at certain times, and the privacy at home was almost too good to be true. He said "you know, you can't imagine what it's like being able to get just the right temperature of water you want, stay in as long as you want to, and not being one or two feet away from a dozen men at any one time". He again remarked how understanding she was of the almost juvenile way he was participating in his first day of real freedom.

The real test was yet to come. How would he fare as far as intimacy? He had serious doubts after all these years, but apprehension never became reality. He did mention that his wife got a little upset when he sprawled out on the bed face down, and just wanted to be alone for a while. She could not figure out why one of the main things he had waited for and missed all those years was being put on hold, now that the perfect opportunity presented itself. He said the hardest thing he had to do all day was to explain to her why he didn't want her in bed with him at the moment. Totally baffled, she waited for what better be a good explanation. Being a height of about 6'5", and having an arm span of about 6 1/2 feet, he pretty much covered the bed.)

He said he knew what she was thinking, or at least had an idea, but in his most convincing voice, he proceeded to tell her that for the last 22 years and more, he has been sleeping on a bed no wider than his shoulders, and that it was like heaven being able to lay on a bed that you can roll all the way over on and still have room to spare. He said that he just wanted to appreciate the moment, knowing there was better to come, and he laid his head down and tried to take it all in. He said from that point on, his day just kept getting better.

He remarked how the little things he did as if he were still in jail, were just second nature. Many habits he had developed, like asking for his food, were strange to her, and hard to put aside at first, especially on the beginning furlows. Old habits die hard, but the nice thing was - she understood

Speaking of habits, I remember an inmate, who is still incarcerated with a life sentence, telling me a funny story one time involving his new arrival in jail. He was young upon arrival, and very unfamiliar with the ways of jail. Once placed in his cell, he noticed the little door at the bottom of the cell door, which was where the officer would slide your tray into you at mealtime. This occurred at the old Eastern State penitentiary in Philadelphia, which has been closed since the early 1970's. Layout and procedures were different there. The way you were fed at times and respect for correctional officers in those days differed quite a bit from the present. Nevertheless, after being there about 2 or 3 days, a C.O. that normally worked the first shift told him that when his food is brought to him, he must run to the back of the cell and face the wall until the tray is in and he leaves. He stressed to him that he must never stand at the door and stare at the C.O. while he slides the food in, or he is in big trouble. Being young, scared, and facing the death penalty, which he had until his sentence was commuted to life at a later time, he took this information seriously. He would be ready the next time.

At the next feeding, he reacted properly. As the C.O. approached, he went running. He stood facing the wall, head down, until the C.O. left. He felt he had done a very good job.

The next meal, same thing. He said he continued this "epitome of respect" reaction for about one week until one day, the food came under the door, and the C.O. yelled "heh, where you going? "Come here, get your food." He said "I can't sir, until you leave." The C.O. then yelled to him to come over to the door. He turned with hesitance, and proceeded cautiously. The C O. happened to be a different one than the one who instructed him to go to the back of the cell. He asked the inmate, "heh, how come you ran to the back of the cell? Here's your food "

He proceeded to tell the C.O. that the other C.O. told him that when the food comes, you must run to the back of your cell, face the wall, and wait until he leaves before getting the tray to eat. He said the C.O. began to laugh, and then it made sense why he would run when the food came. The C.O. left him with a good meal (the food was much better then so they say) and a good piece of advise, "Son, don't believe everything you hear in jail." The inmate then realized that he had truly been duped.

There are things though that are very believable in jail, involving and coming from inmates. Drugs, jailhouse wine, sex, weapons, scams of various kinds, are all very believable. I laughed when I heard about the inmate that had a VCR in his cell hooked up to the TV.! I later found out that it was one that was missing from the school, and was part of a business venture. He apparently was one that enjoyed watching X-rated movies or worse, triple X films - and was charging admission to other inmates to view the flicks! Shame on you, Mr. Movieman.

Or, how about the inmate, who by the way was allegedly one of only six to ever escape by going over the wall at SCI-Graterford, who used the rope that was sewn into his mattress for about one year before the planned escape! Even more amazing was the fact that it happened to be the bottom rope off of the boxing ring, and he managed to get this 80 foot rope all the way back to his cell and coiled into his mattress until needed. From what I heard, it did delay the upcoming boxing match, and must have provided some great back support until he left - or should we say, decided to leave.

Stories like these, even though unique in their own context, are common throughout inmate life. It seems someone is always thinking up a way to get something they should not have or do something they should not be doing. This is very understandable, considering the time they have to think about these things. As many people realize, if as much effort would have been exerted into getting an education and abiding to the rules of society, the jails would not be nearly as full.

This brings to mind a story I heard a number of years ago pertaining to illiteracy. It was told to me by the cell mate of an illiterate man, who acted as the go-between for the subject and his wife. Since the subject, who we will call Joe, was illiterate, he needed to have letters written and read for him in order to correspond. This is not uncommon in jail, and involves more people than one might imagine. Nevertheless, as letters would come in for Joe, his cell mate would open them and read them to him. We are not talking business mail here. We're talking personal, intimate, coercive, lusty and downright steamy stationary! The cell mate revealed to me that he himself had been locked up for quite a while, and rarely if ever received letters like these! He said he would read these to Joe, and watch him grow more excited with each line. He wanted to tell Joe that he felt almost as if he knew the girl, but didn't think it was appropriate, or healthy for their friendship! Vivid descriptions, graphics, desires, intentions, and feelings, all right there at his fingertips!

He finished by saying that he felt bad for Joe, having to correspond for him in those circumstances. He admitted getting very excited himself at times, but never letting Joe know it.

Laughing boldly, with seemingly sinister tone attached, he said "heh, half the fun is reading the letters, but the best part is writing back!!!

One other story, with some similarity to "Joe's" happened to take place as a result of an error in record keeping (certainly not uncommon in the D.O.C.) For those who do not know, the inmates number being recorded precisely means everything. If off by one digit (of which there are only six) the inmate could lose a visit, a Dr.'s appointment, medication, or something else of importance. This includes none other than one's mail.

As mentioned earlier, the mail room processes many thousands of pieces of mail in a day's or week's time, and whether you receive what is coming to you or not depends on that all important six-digit number assigned to you and only you. Anyway, somehow, the man in this story began to receive beautiful love letters from a certain someone whom he had never met. He tried his hardest to remember if he had known her on the outside, or met her through a friend, or even in the prison visiting room. To no avail, he gave up, but continued to enjoy the letters and respond accordingly. As we all know, if the name was wrong consistently, we would assume it was the wrong name, right number or vice versa. In this case, she would put the number on, and throughout the letters, references were made in the way of "Babe", "honey", and other pet words used between her and her husband. After about two months of this, the wonderful letters stopped. Ironically, another inmate on this man's cell block happened to be talking about not receiving any letters from his wife in almost two months, but was ecstatic after receiving one recently. He was more than anxious to respond, hoping to resolve the problem of not receiving his previous letters.

The inmate who had been receiving the letters told me he just didn't have the heart to tell the man what had been happening, partially because he enjoyed the correspondence so much. He was glad for the guy that the mix-up was straightened out, but in a way, was very disappointed.

After reading these letters and getting his hopes up, he figured the visiting room was going to be the next step. He said "man, after reading those letters, I couldn't wait to meet that girl!"

He said his main regret was that number one, he was in jail, and the big disappointment was number two, she was married.

There are many stories of violence in jail also. Things like violence and escapes - or at least attempted ones - are common to the jail environment, and can be expected to happen on the spur of the moment. Violence may occur due to a bad exchange of words, a stolen article, a bad drug deal, unpaid debts, infringement on one's time or property, or unfulfilled promises. The list of incidents that can cause a disturbance in jails is never ending.

I can recall an incident where bleach was thrown in a man's eyes and face as he responded to a tap on his shoulder to see who it was. This man turned out to be a thief that had stolen a radio from the throwers' cell. I also recall a very similar incident, where gasoline from the small engine repair shop was used instead of bleach, and as the victim stumbled around with temporary blindness, he was beaten with a padlock concealed in a sock (called a lock-in-a-sock).

I can well remember a laundry cart half-full with clean laundry being rushed down the main corridor by four inmates as fast as possible, all yelling for help for the blood covered inmate lying down inside who had just been stabbed a dozen times or more. The hospital personnel with the gurney did not respond fast enough, so the laundry cart made the next best mode of transportation. I can also well remember the inmate who was found beaten and stabbed lying under his bunk in his cell. It was revealed later that he had not carried out an order given to him by another inmate who was the leader of an organization he belonged to. I can well recall inmates who were victims of love triangles - two different men pursuing the same third man - one was just a bit more jealous and aggressive than the other. Whether it be an all male or an all female jail - domestic quarrels are a fact of life, and very dangerous situations at times.

I can still remember the call going out for a potential hanging on the block. As I was finishing up some work just around the corner from the dispensary area, I walked by the door and saw a very purple looking body lying on the stretcher. With closer investigation, I noticed it was an inmate who I had talked to many times in the past. Found hanging in his cell by the bedsheet tied to an overhead radiator, the deep ridges and discoloration around his neck and head surely spoke of his desperation and lack of interest in living any longer. With a sentence of life plus many years after to remain in jail, and no hope of leaving due to the nature of his case, he apparently felt that it was too much to deal with any longer. Along the same line, I can still recall various inmates over the years being rescued as they bled out in their cells from self-inflicted wounds to the wrists, neck, and various other areas of their body. There are also those who entertain the ingestion of nails, razor blades, glass, pencils, or whatever else they can get their hands on. Some desiring to die, some desiring only attention, and some going a little too far and dying accidentally.

These are real jail stories. Stories of people who were abusers and later were abused themselves. Stories of people who were perpetrators, and later became victims of perpetrators. Stories of people who preyed on society, and now themselves are preyed upon. Stories of people who were always followers and never leaders. And then there are those who just decided to give up.

And the stories go on and on. Some more sad than funny, and some not fit for print (if using all the expletives used in the real setting.) Jail house stories are merely a recollection of the true character and nature of inmates. Some people find it hard to appreciate any humor, or redeeming qualities associated with inmates. Viewed by society as disgusting, incorrigible, sub-human beings, some inmates tend to assume the role of underachiever quite easily, and hold onto it for dear life.

Objectively speaking, I think these stories tend to reflect a side of inmates many people fail to realize they have in some cases. The lack of good judgement and moral fiber, accompanied by bad decision making, does not negate or deny the presence of emotion, feelings, sense of humor, or understanding.

Many employees act like they cannot stand inmates at times, and tend to talk about them like the rest of society does. The funny thing is that some of those same employees cannot wait to get to the work the next day for another helping of intrigue offered in the daily diet of prison life. After the meal, complete with cake, the icing is usually all worth it - yet another good story to tell - to friends, family and curiosity seekers.

As an inmate once said to me sarcastically, and so appropriate is the saying .... "to know us, is to love us!"....

Inmate Writes

Many people are intrigued by the things some inmates say and do. These so-called "things" are really nothing more than the everyday words and actions of people that exist in society everywhere, but gathering numbers of people who have contributed to the criminal element of society and placing them together under one roof seems to heighten the sense of intrigue. Many of us who work in the jail setting have experienced the "lust" for prison stories when attending social functions of various kinds. When people know or hear of the fact that you work in a jail, they many times cannot fight the urge to ask for a prison story, or seek information concerning something they have read about "your jail". I've run across that at the supermarket, the bank, the hospital, and in countless situations with family and friends. Inmates do not realize at times how popular they really are.

Questions in general about the "badness" of inmates, their personalities, their crimes, and the old "aren't you afraid to work there" types usually dominate the conversation. A person can be the life of the party just telling stories and sharing facts about prison. More often than not, a friend or acquaintance will tell you about something they have heard, or ask a question that leads you into the conversation. It is hard for me to stand idly by and not comment, especially if the information is not accurate. The ones that make me laugh are those who will ask if I know a certain inmate, wait for my reaction, and then proceed to tell me that they are related or a close friend. Those "lead in" questions also tend to open the door to general prison discussions. Situations like those are the main reason I decided to write this chapter. I thought it would be interesting to the average reader to see a few statistics and read the actual comments made by the inmates themselves. Inmates do not usually have the opportunity to voice their opinions to a large number of people, so I put together a small questionnaire and got the responses of some inmates chosen at random. The identity of these men is totally unknown, which opened the door to more honesty, and less intimidation and apprehension in answering the questions. Conducting the survey this way also relieved the need for consent forms and massive writing on my part. The responses were excellent, and very candid as I desired them to be. In some cases, the answers to some of the questions varied greatly, whereas others were much as anticipated.

To begin with, the average age of all people surveyed was 38 years old. The youngest being 20 years old, and the oldest being 58 years old. The most extreme in age that I have ever heard of here was 14 years old in the youthful group, and 94 years old in the senior group. Due to an increase in juvenile crime and crimes committed by young adults, the jail population is actually shifting to a younger group overall. A large number of the new receptions I see every day are approximately 18 to 30 years of age. This is bringing increased awareness and concern to the older more "seasoned" prisoner, due to the decrease in values and morals accompanying this new younger criminal element.

With regard to sentencing, slightly less than 50% of all people surveyed were lifers, having been sentenced to spend the rest of their natural life in jail, unless the laws governing life sentences in Pennsylvania change in the future. Approximately 36% had minimum sentences of ten years or more, and about 30% had a minimum sentence of less than ten years. Regarding extremes, I know of one inmate that has a 140 year minimum to 280 year maximum for multiple robberies, and others that have two years or less, for parole violations.

Whether the sentence they received was just, unjust, fair, or unfair - 56% said they felt their sentence was unjust, and about 29% stated their sentence was unfair. Some of the reasons given are as follows:

a) Bad counsel.
b) Falsified evidence-judge ignored the facts and evidence.
c) Prejudice on the part of the District Attorney, Judge, or Jury.
d) Falsely identified.
e) No attorney; defended self.
f) Sentence too extreme for the crime.

110

g) False evidence presented.
h) Crime was unintentional.
i) Simply did not hurt anyone.
j) Was only an accomplice.
k) Discrimination.
l) Killed in self defense.
m) Was framed.
n) Post traumatic stress syndrome.
o) Declared innocence.
p) Could have gotten less time to achieve a better result.
q) Had no memory of the past crime.
r) Because I was found guilty on my past crimes and not what I was being tried for at this time.

One inmate stated that "justice is motivated by money, ambition, and politics. The prosecution used its resources to obtain an unjust verdict." As far as receiving a fair or just sentence, approximately 15% of all surveyed made this claim. Most of these people stated similar reasons as follows:

a) Fair-due to the number of crimes I committed - I was really blessed by God only to receive the little amount of time that I did.
b) Fair - due to past criminal record.
c) Fair - what I did was wrong.
d) Just - I violated my parole.
e) Just - because I did rob these people.
f) Just - I committed a crime.
g) Just - we deserve more than that (the sentence) for our sins.
h) Fair - they could have given me more.
i) Just - Fourth conviction for violent offense (robbery). I squandered opportunities and ran to convenience. Society had to do something.

It is interesting to note, not knowing any of these people by the survey, that the ones who thought they had a fair and/or just trial all show some remorse and repentance for their actions and admit some guilt, while most who made claims of unfair or unjust seem to want to immediately try and shift the burden and blame on someone or something else. Sadly enough, many of these individuals will remain angry and bitter toward the system, themselves, and the rest of the world until they admit their guilt, if there is any, and ask for forgiveness.

Next, two questions were asked concerning the way they were tried. I wanted to know if they had a jury trial, and if they received a fair trial (by jury or judge). About 21 % stated they had a fair trail, and most of them were the ones who said they received a fair or just sentence. About 65% said they had a trial by jury. Interestingly enough, most who were tried by a jury were the ones who said they did not receive a fair trail, as opposed to trial by a judge. This could possibly say something about the fairness of a judge compared to the fairness of a jury.

I was curious as to the number of inmates that did time before this present sentence they are now serving. I also wanted to know where the previous sentence or sentences were served as far as state, county, or federal facility. Of all surveyed, just less than one half did not serve time prior to this sentence. This told me that a little over one half of all these inmates had served previous time and were no strangers to the jail system. Approximately 50% of all who served previous time did so in a county facility, while about 44% did so in a state facility. Only about 6% served time in federal prison before this present sentence. Nevertheless, what does this say about the effectiveness of our system on cutting down recidivism when 50% or more are returning to jail again?

This leads into the next question asked which involves parole. I was curious as to how many, out of all surveyed, were ever on parole. Approximately 46% said they were, and slightly over half of those were parole violators. It is interesting to note that almost all of those who violated parole stated that they got along well with their parole officers, and as many or slightly more stated that their parole officer was fair.

I bluntly and openly asked about guilt or innocence, which as most people know is a seemingly secondary factor in most courtrooms and many lawyers minds. It was stated as follows:

"By all legal standards, are you innocent or guilty of the crime(s) for which you were convicted?" About 45% of all surveyed said they were guilty, and of course about 55% stated they were innocent. Included in the innocent bunch were a few that were wavering between guilt and innocence due to circumstances, which in their minds meant that they were about 50% guilty and 50% innocent! (Most of these were first or second degree murder cases.) A few felt they were innocent because the police allegedly lied or the District Attorney presented false evidence. One felt he was innocent, not because he did not kill the person, but because he was only sixteen years old with no police record at the time of the killing, so he feels that he really is not guilty. Two others felt that they were only 50% guilty due to both people being killed at the same time, and the sentence being too excessive for the crimes. Some feel that this is like saying a woman is only 50% pregnant due to circumstances beyond her control!

As reality has it, no matter what the circumstances, a crime that has taken place had to have occurred somewhere, sometime, somehow, and by someone. Circumstances of any degree should only tend to help determine the severity of the sentence, and not alter the guilt of committing the actual crime. In other words, if you committed the crime with malice or not, with intent or not, or with remorse or not, you are still guilty. Unfortunately, certain elements of the legal system in this country through practice of intellectual deceit to varying degrees, have helped to convince great numbers of people, especially those of the criminal element and with violent criminal tendencies, that guilt can be reduced or even eliminated due to "circumstances". Plea bargaining is a common practice that tends to send out this very message - a message that says in some cases that just because you did the crime, does not necessarily mean you will do all the time, or in some cases, any of it. It is understood why this is done, usually to gain information needed or to obtain a confession of some sort, but the message it sends out is one that some feel is not conducive with punishment for the entire crime.

Next, I asked all surveyed if they felt any remorse about the crime(s) that brought them to prison. As a follow-up to that

113

question, I asked who they felt the victim was in their case. About 65°% stated they did feel remorse to some degree for what they did, and 35°% stated they did not. A fair number of the non-remorse people also stated that they themselves were the victims. Some said themselves, plus one or more other people were the victims. The majority stated that others were the victims as follows:

a) My friend.
b) The man that was shot.
c) Two young women.
d) A stranger (many gave this answer).
e) The deceased.
f) The Commonwealth (mentioned a few times).
g) Both families.
h) Both families and victims.
i) Not sure.
j) Several.
k) The neighbor.
l) A close friend.
m) An old friend.
n) My mother.
o) My family.
p) Society (mentioned a few times).
q) The people at the scene.
r) The store (mentioned a few times).
s) An acquaintance.
t) The victims and the Commonwealth.
u) A female.
v) A series of drug dealers.
w) A police officer - but really me.
x) Property and Me.
y) Me.

Many of these answers were duplicated a number of times, sometimes worded a little differently. One that stuck out as a little amusing but possibly very true was given by an inmate who stated he had no remorse for the crime, but did admit he robbed the store. (which will go unnamed). He stated that "if it were not for drugs, I would not be in jail, and I'm only bad when using drugs". Again, possibly very true. He went on to say that his sentence was unjust, even though he admitted he was guilty, due to the fact that "he never got a break from the courts like the young white boys." There is no way of knowing, but one may assume this man is a minority, and apparently feels he was treated in a prejudicial manner. Again, possibly very true. As we all know, the system is and always will be capable of practicing in this manner, whether any of us likes it or not.

The next question was, "Do you believe in the laws by which we are governed?" As I anticipated, less than half of all surveyed said yes - about 38% to be a little more specific. Approximately 56% stated they do not believe in the laws by which we are governed, which probably contributes to the fact that more people are coming to jail than ever before. A few stated they believed in some of the laws but not all, and one man said that this is a very ambiguous question. One of particular interest was a man who stated "not anymore" to the question. The inmate happens to be serving two life sentences plus another 55 to 110 years after those. In many cases, when sentences like this are imposed, they will run concurrently, or all at the same time. In this case, they are "running wild" (jail slang) or consecutively, one after the other. This means technically after two lifetimes, plus another 55 years served, he then has a chance for parole! It is not difficult to understand why he gave the answer that he did.

Speaking of stiff sentences, the next question asked was "Do you feel that stiffer sentencing is a deterrent to crime?" This is a loaded question to ask inmates, since the majority of them feel that even with the knowledge that they could go to jail if convicted for committing a crime, it still would not stop many of them from doing what they did. Approximately 90% of all surveyed said stiffer sentencing would not be a deterrent, while the remaining 10% said that it would be. The general thinking behind this is that many crimes are committed on spur of the moment reactions, and incarceration is not at the forethought of the reactions. As far as premeditated murders, planned robberies, or any other thought-out crime, the possibility of penalty consideration is present, but many times the state of mind negates the probability of this forethought occurring. The aftershock of a large sentence, or any sentence in some cases, always occurs too late, and hindsight can be and often is a tough teacher. I, and others that I have talked to, have often wondered if the majority of inmates choose to take this stand on sentencing in hopes that stiffer penalities will not be imposed, just in case they do not decide to change their lifestyles, lest they are convicted for committing a crime again sometime. It is hard for me to personally imagine, that if the man mentioned earlier with the two life sentences and another 55 to 110 years to follow, knew beyond a shadow of a doubt he would receive such a penalty if convicted, that he would still pursue his criminal life and activity as he did.

Next, concerning deterrents and all that surrounds them, this question was asked: "If the state were to execute everyone who is sentenced to death, do you think it would be a deterrent to violent crime?" A very definite "No" was received with about 90% of all surveyed stating that it would not deter violent crime. The comments and justifications for their answers are both interesting and informative. They are as follows:

1) No, because people don't think before they act. Some people act on justice, and most don't.
2) No, because people do violent crimes on the spur of the moment or by accident. Pros do murder with the thought that they won't get caught.
3) No, because people now are more violent than I've ever seen in my lifetime.
4) No, because it hasn't been a deterrent yet. Two wrongs do not make a right.
5) No, because statistics say that crimes will always occur.
6) No, because "thou shalt not kill".
7) No, because most violent crime is not premeditated, and generally the victim and the perpetrator are acquainted and anger overcomes logic.

8) No, it was never a deterrent in the past so surely in the future it would not work. No one intends on getting caught.
9) No, things are real bad on the outside, and there are way too many drugs.
10) No, because there's always someone to take their place.
11) No, because crime is deeply rooted in todays' social problems between the haves and have-nots.
12) No, killing does not justify or bring change.
13) No, never has.
14) No, it just isn't.
15) No, you can't determine someone's future by someone's indirect past.
16) No, people are not afraid to commit crimes because they believe what they are doing is right.
17) No, if there are 1,000 people on death row and they kill all of them, 995 would be the wrong one.
18) No, killing people is a violation of the law of God, and will not stop people from violent crimes.
19) No, because I just don't think it would, because most cons are not all that violent.
20) No, other people would still commit crimes.
21) No, those determined to engage in these types of crimes do so regardless of any deterrent because of the very nature of the individual.
22) No, I don't believe in an eye for an eye, because it would not bring the person back.
23) No, I don't believe in the death penalty and it is not up to me, it is up to Allah to decide.
24) No, people are going to be people, until it happens to everyone that thinks that they have the best plan in breaking the law.
25) Yes, because people would think about taking another life before acting out against the community. Less people would be killed for their property or possessions if the criminal thought he would die instead of living out the remainder of his life behind bars.
26) Yes, because you know that the state is taking a life.

27) No, look at all the people on death row.

26) No, executing someone only makes it worse because now if the person had or was thinking about putting their weapon down, they would use it because they will probably be executed anyway.

29) No, the most prolific criminals are protected by their jobs and positions in government and law enforcement in government, and law enforcement agencies.

30) Yes, it would make people think twice about taking a life.

31) No, people don't do things planning to be found out-they do things planning to get away with it.

32) No, for two reasons. First, two wrongs do not make a right; my death will not and could not bring back the man I killed. Second, I did not say to myself "if I kill this guy or someone else, I am going to die - or get the death sentence." My killing was an accident. I did not want or mean to kill anyone.

33) No, eye for an eye won't work, and if people know they will die for a violent crime, they won't be taken alive.

34) No, most people don't intentionally set out to kill someone, and while they are responsible for their actions, you can't hold them responsible for someone's unintentional death.

35) No, the economical structure in our society purposely creates situations of imagined wants, etc., so we as a people always have created needs instead of depending on our abilities bestowed by the Heavenly Father.

36) No, it has never been a deterrent in our entire history.

37) No, although some inmates on death row may be guilty to some degree, most of the accused in the Pennsylvania prison systems are there through selective and vindictive prosecution. No concrete evidence. Violent crime has always been, even before our time. What on earth could any rational thinking person signify to conclude that somehow we are going to cease violent crime today? It's an evil ploy!

38) No, people will continue to commit violent crimes

(murder) regardless of the consequences. In the heat of anger or passion one doesn't think of the consequences of his or her actions.

39) No, there are some times you must do things regardless of consequences.

Well, there you have it. A small but interesting collection of some of the most duplicated and individual answers and opinions to one of the most controversial questions in the criminal justice system today - right from the pens of the inmates. I would only conclude by saying that possibly these statements might help to sway your opinion on this matter one way or the other, in addition to already gathered facts and opinions that you the reader may have had previously. It is interesting to note that many of the people that gave 'yes" answers did not comment as to why, while many who said "no" certainly did express their thoughts and feelings, as you have just read.

Next, I was curious as to the approximate percentage of C.O.'s the inmates feel are suited for the prison environment, and do a good job while on duty. About 45% of all surveyed said they felt about 10% were suited for the job. About 25% of all surveyed stated they felt that 25% to 50% were suited for the job. About 12% said that 10% to 25% were suited, and about 12% said that 50% to 75% were suited. Approximately 5% of all surveyed said they felt that 75% to 100% of all officers were suited for the job. One of the inmates was very blunt and showed no mercy by stating that 0% were suited for the job. Other than the fact that he has a life sentence, we detect a slight feeling of bitterness toward correctional officers and the authority they hold.

I thought it would be interesting to know how many surveyed ever did time in any other institution(s) and what the best and worst things were about those institution(s). About 45% of all surveyed served time in other jails, and about 55% did not. As far as the best things about the other jails, some stated the following;

a) Nothing.

b) Better staff.
c) The food.
d) Cleaner environment.
e) Better housing.
f) Better treatment.
g) The good time policy.
h) They are all the same.
i) Order.
j) My short stay.
k) I left before I died.

(The Good Time policy, where applied, helps to reduce time served by offering credit for good conduct, educational courses, etc. Presently, there is no good time policy in effect in the State of Pennsylvania).

And now for some of the worst things in other institutions. They were stated as follows:

a) Lockdown.
b) Security.
c) Racism/racial tension.
d) Rapes all the time.
e) The dorm settings.
f) The fact that I can't go back (stuck here).
g) Everything.
h) Just being there!
i) Disregard for my humanity.
j) Far from home.

One other comment was that "they're all the same".

Next, I asked "have you ever just sat and thought about the crime(s) for which you were convicted?" About 95% of all surveyed said yes, with the remaining five percent saying no. How could you possibly avoid it? Immediately following that question, I asked "are you a better person since you have been in prison?" Please explain. The answers most common were as follows:

a) Yes, because I think more rationally than before.
b) Yes, I was a drinker and sometime drug abuser. I have been straight now for 18 of my 20 years in prison, and educated myself.
c) Yes, because if it were not for drugs, I would not be in here. I'm only bad when I'm using drugs.
d) No, because the system doesn't work.
e) Yes, (no comment).
f) Yes, my understanding and spirituality has increased due to the fact that I have had the time for self examination.
g) Yes, I stopped drugs and only get violent when threatened.
h) Yes, I am now educated.
i) Yes, I used the system to educate and improve all my skills in a positive manner
j) No, because I am not guilty.
k) No, I still have the same thoughts and desires.
l) Yes, because I want out, and I know God is real more than ever.
m) Yes, I know that crime doesn't pay.
n) Yes, because of therapy.
o) Yes, because of N.A. meetings.
p) Yes, I have been in jail nearly 17 years, and I believe I am a better person in that I have grown morally, academically, spiritually, socially and economically.
q) Yes, I am more reasonable now.
r) Yes, Now I am straight and I realize everything I did wrong.
s) No, I was a good person before I came to jail.
t) I've given my life to Christ Jesus, whom through his divine word have shown me a new way of life, a new way to think, and that trusting in Him gives me that everlasting peace in Him.
u) No, no comment.
v) Yes, I try to improve my attitude.
w) Yes, I know that nothing in life comes easy.
x) No, this system creates anger.
y) Yes and no, I am a better person due to the time I can

spend with God and rely on Him to lead me. I am not better for gaining any skills because it takes too long to get into a decent job or school.

z) Yes and no, I don't see how imprisonment would make me a better person, however, I now recognize untapped potentials and talents which if recognized early on, would have given me a greater advantage in life.

Many parallel answers were received to this question, many saying the same thing only worded a little differently. Many commented on the awareness that imprisonment brought to them as far as the value of life, the clearness of mind once getting off drugs and alcohol, the value of living daily in a legal and moral manner, and the change in their life with a confirmed belief in God. I felt that all the comments were excellent, but due to space limitation I could not list all of them verbatim. I did list the ones that were within the same. concept, and any outstanding or unique ones were noted. The unfortunate thing is that incarceration has and does only create a temporary realization of life values in some cases, and does not provide a lasting effect as does dependence on God and following His principles and laws.

The next question was simple and to the point. It reads as follows: "Are you under any stress in prison?" Only 75% of all surveyed said yes. One would imagine that 90 to 100 percent would say yes to this question, considering the environment and living conditions. Obviously, what is stressful to some or most people is not the case with everyone, if indeed they are telling the truth. In conjunction with prison stress, I asked "how do you feel about doing time?" Some of the answers were as follows:

1) I don't like it one bit.
2) Pretty bad, lonely.
3) I hate it.
4) We must pay for our crimes if guilty. It's hell if you are innocent.
5) Only an insane human being would not be dissatisfied with this madness.
6) It's not a prior feeling.

7) Real bad.
8) As everyone else, I want to be free from this place.
9) I am often depressed. I am confused. I am destroyed. I am deprived of my humanity. My heart is severly aching.
10) I feel that the state is spending a whole lot of money to feed and house me, but is getting yanked by their own system because they refuse to rehab the felon in his needed area.
11) Bad.
12) I feel as though it did some good as far as me making more clear decisions concerning my life.
13) Bitter.
14) I don't like it especially when I didn't commit the crime.
15) I'm certainly not happy about it, but I've learned to adjust and try to make the best of the situation. I try to use the time to my advantage.
16) F ---d up.
17) I feel it did some good for my life.
18) No sweat.
19) I hate it.
20) It's hard.
21) Tired.
22) Gotta do it, no choices were given.
23) I feel real depressed.
24) I hate being away from my loved ones.
25) If you really thought there was more than one way to feel about it, you wouldn't ask.
26) Hopeless.
27) Frustrated, impotent, humiliated at times. Most times I try not to feel anything.
28) It S---s.
29) You got to stay alert.
30) It is an absolute waste of money and manpower.
31) Terrible.
32) A criminal should be punished, but not forever if they have tried and have changed.
33) Mixed feelings. I do not deny what I did, but also must

hope to get out one day. We all must have some kind of
hope to go on living. If there were no hope in the world,
how do you think the world would be?
34) Bad, because I did not see my daughter grow up.
35) Doing time is one of the most useless things you can do.
36) No one wants to be locked up, guilty or not.
37) Not too thrilled. The social deprivation leaves heinous
scars; and results in subtle and unforseen reprecussions.
38) I try not "2" feel.

Many said they hated it. Many said it was lonely,
depressing, etc. A few even used very descriptive terms and
adjectives to say how they felt, which I gave a little hint of. In
conclusion, I think the general consensus is the same on this
question.
Next, I asked "what was your feeling or impression of the
state prison when you first arrived here?" Some of the most
common answers were as follows:

1) Wow! Everything was so huge.
2) Cold, unnecessary waiting.
3) Physical hell, totally equipped with white and black
devils.
4) A place to get out of as quickly as possible.
5) Scared.
6) I am in for the trial of my life.
7) The same loneliness that still abides here for lack of
family to associate with.
8) The worst thing that has ever happened to me.
9) This is hell!
10) I was ready for it from all I've heard.
11) Bitterness because of an unjust judicial system. I viewed
the prison as just another level of an unfair system.
12) It needs a lot of work on it as far as cleanliness,
guidelines.
13) I felt that I would be lost and forgotten here. I was
impressed (in a negative sense) with the size and the

noise. I also felt I was entering a place for the living dead.

14) Weird.

15) Messed up.

16) Afraid.

17) Big place.

18) I felt hurt and stripped of all my rights.

19) Wow!

20) Can't remember.

21) I arrived in "86", it was a nightmare, but I adapted.

22) I was impressed to be in a community where everyone functioned on the ability to stay in his own place.

23) Bad experience. Like modern day slavery.

24) Amazed that I'd see all the people that I haven't seen in a long time.

25) Too many people.

26) Very unorganized.

27) Cold, hard, and rotten.

28) Scary and intimidating.

29) A very inhuman environment that deteriates the moral fibers of all concerned. It serves no real purpose.

30) Scared to death.

31) I was dazed and confused.

32) Extremely violent.

33) Cruel and unusual.

34) A nightmare.

35) It's like a rat hole. Bad food, bad people. People who work here are low scum, 50%of them.

36) I was a little afraid, but I don't have any complaints about the prison per se. The Lord God helps one to cope and follow the rules.

37) I'll do what I have to do to get out, but most of all stay out of things that don't concern me.

38) Men were here and people mind their own business - It wasn't a lot of the say B.S. going on.

39) A place just made to keep people away from society.

40) Unorganized, poorly trained guards, personal apperance very poor.

41) No feeling.

Life in prison is handled very differently by each and every inmate. Goals, standards, and morals differ with each and everyone who is incarcerated. This brings us to the question "what do you do to survive in prison?" Some interesting and similar answers were as follows:

1) Read and stay away form people who are not trying to go home.
2) Work in the greenhouse.
3) Watch television, work, exercise, and play my trumpet.
4) Work.
5) Continue my faith in Allah and continue to work towards freedom, along with going to school.
6) Study.
7) Work, read, watch TV., exercise, and try to avoid trouble.
8) Religion.
9) Tutor inmates, talk to younger inmates and try to understand the nature of people.
10) Work, read, and pray five times a day.
11) Write, engage in meaningful conversation, laugh, and joke.
12) Go to school.
13) Work on my case.
14) Exercise.
15) Art work.
16) Read, write letters, make phone calls.
17) Have faith and try to do God's will.
18) Go to N.A. meetings.
19) I mind my own business and do not talk to the guards.
20) Hide.
21) Religion - Islam.
22) I exist only for the day of my release. Also I pray.
23) I learned the system's jurisprudence and used it back on them.

24) I mind my own business and participate in positive activities.
25) I trust and depend on God to bring me through and execute justice.
26) Creative writing
27) Play music in the Institutional band.

Most, if not all, said that they either work, watch T.V., or exercise. Some of the comments did not make perfect sense, but nevertheless were from the heart. Many varying combinations of all the above were noted.

Next, as far as survival in jail is concerned, I asked "Was your life ever threatened in prison?" If so, explain. Approximately 62% said no, and about 38% said yes. Again, some similar answers were received along with some unique ones, as follows:

a) Yes, and I worked it out without any complications.
b) Yes, An insane inmate thought I was watching him, so he stabbed me 14 times without warning.
c) Yes. I talked to the guy and used ethics, intelligence, integrity, empathy on both sides and prayed.
d) Yes, I got myself a weapon and kept a close eye on the person who threatened me.
e) Yes, I handled it myself with violence.
f) Yes, I threatened him back.
g) Yes, with alertness, I still wait for the threat to be fulfilled.
h) Yes, I reported it to the C.O.
i) Yes, they took my clothes.
j) Yes, you never know how someone is feeling.
k) Yes, I handled it myself.
l) Yes, I handled it sometimes by talking and negotiations, but most times with physical violence.
m) Yes, my life is threatened every second I spend in prison. I try to be conscious of the environment, the different personality types, my health, and keep faith in God.

n) Yes, the staff attempted to let me die from sugar diabetes. I was graced by God and pulled through.
o) Yes, I just walked away and let the problem rest in God's hands.
p) Yes, I let it pass because of where we are at.
q) Yes, I used the skills I was brought into this world with.
r) Yes, I hurt the person who issued the threat.
s) Yes, lawsuit.

Many times life in jail may include carrying and using a weapon of various sorts. Some have seen weapons, but never had occasion to use them personally, which leads us to ask "have you personally ever seen or used a weapon in prison?" If yes, explain." Approximately 70% stated that they never saw or used a weapon in jail. Out of the remaining 30% that stated they did, some of the explanations were as follows:

a) I have seen many weapons in prison, but never used one.
b) I have seen knives they have found here.
c) I have seen zip guns, knives, pipes, locks in socks, acid, gas, pipe bombs, and flamables thrown on people.
d) I have one myself to stay alive.
e) You see them every day.
f) I've seen dozens of weapons - anything can be used as a weapon.
g) During shakedowns, they are thrown out of the windows
h) Can't explain.
i) I've seen numerous weapons of all types during my incarceration, held by some of the people that hung around with me in my earlier years.
j) I've seen them from time to time.
k) I was stabbed with a shank.
l) I would rather not explain.
m) Weapons are a part of all violent environments.
n) I had to knock a guy in the head who was attacking me.

Again, many responses were similar to the ones listed, so we picked the most common for the sake of space.

The subject of crime in jail is very interesting, considering the fact that now the once perpetrators are now the victims in and among all the other perpetrators. I was curious as to how many inmates in the survey were ever victims themselves of crime. If they said yes to the question, I asked for a brief explanation. Approximately 56% of all surveyed said they were never victims, and about 44% stated they were victims of crime at some point. Some even feel that incarceration made them a victim. The comments were as follows:

a) Beaten by Philadelphia police.
b) My cell was robbed
c) My car was stolen.
d) I got shot when some guys tried to rob me.
e) No comment.
f) I was robbed.
g) I was robbed and assaulted.
h) I was robbed and my wife was raped.
i) I got shot before.
j) My mother and I were robbed.
k) I was physically assaulted and robbed on the streets of Philadelphia.
l) I am unjustly in prison.
m) I am in prison suffering a prison life for a crime I did not commit, if a crime was indeed committed.
n) Robbed at gunpoint.
o) I'm victim cus I was a Black man.
p) Carjacked, gang beaten, house robbed.
q) I had a car stolen, my tools taken, and my tape player stolen out of my car. I also have things stolen in here (jail).
r) The Commonwealth of Pennsylvania has victimized me by fabricating evidence to cause me to be imprisoned.

Because prison is the kind of place that it is, I next asked what they thought were the worst and best things about the prison they are currently serving time in. They listed the best things as follows:

a) Nothing that I could think of.
b) The practice of your religion.
c) Nothing.
d) It gives me a little freedom to move about and to practice my faith and educational program.
e) Some people deserve to be here.
f) The education department.
g) No comment.
h) No one is related to me.
i) Knowing that I will get out.
j) I am able to sleep at night and be thankful for waking up in the morning.
k) It's closer to Phildelphia.
l) The music program.
m) Close to home.
n) The two Deputies, the Superintendent, and Director of Treatment do seem to care a little.
o) Good programs.
p) The chapel.
q) Visits, phone calls, mail.
r) I've been trusted enough by the administration to be placed in a job outside the walls.
s) The freedom inside.
t) Jobs.
u) Working outside on the Farm.
v) The library.
w) Awaiting my parole date.
x) The N.A. and A.A. meetings.
y) You can go to school and do a lot of studying about yourself.
z) I can't decide.

The worst things were listed as follows:

a) Everything.
b) Lack of educational programs.
c) The food is always cold.

d) The men are still allowed to destroy themselves with drugs, using, and selling.
e) No comment.
f) The food.
g) The paperwork for inmates release.
h) There is no one related to the people who sent me here.
i) I can't leave when I want to.
j) Healthcare.
k) Too many things to list.
l) The food - and the boss steals from his workers smokes that were given for outside work done.
m) Overcrowding, which cause more stress.
n) The walls are too thick.
o) The C.O.'s.
p) Food, staff, and too many young inmates.
q) Petty guards and the petty rules they enforce (example, locked in cell for 15 days for cursing).
r) Noise and ignorance.
s) Dirty, rules are not enforced. Too many "teacher's pets".
t) Violence.
u) Just being here.
v) Guards are stupid, and inmates are more stupid.
w) Two in a cell.
x) Robberies and assaults.
y) The kids in here.
z) Refusing to give a man a chance to make parole or helping him to better himself so he won't come back.

Now that you have heard from the inmates concerning jail life and their feelings about the environment and the justice system, it would only be fair to look at their personal lives and feelings a little closer. I asked a series of questions along these lines beginning with the following:

a) Did you ever own a home? Rent a home? Rent an apartment?

About 42% of all surveyed said they owned a home sometime in their life. Approximately 39% stated that they rented a house or apartment, and about 19% neither owned or rented a living area during their lifetime.

b) Do you have any children? If so, what are their ages?

About 65% of all surveyed had children, and about 35% said they did not. The ages of the children ranged from 2 years of age to 34 years of age. Some had as few as one child and one stated he had nine children, ranging from ages ten to thirty-four. The average per family was about two children, but three or four was not uncommon in a few cases.

c) Are you married? If your answer is yes, is it common-law, or legal?
    1. Are you legally separated?
    2. Divorced?

If your answer is number 1 or 2, is it due to incarceration, or other reasons?

Unfortunately, the findings to this question were not very accurate, due to the question not being answered properly and entirely by some. Of the ones who did answer correctly, it appeared that about 30% of the men were married, with about 5% of those being separated. It appeared that about 12% of those married were legally married as opposed to commonlaw marriage. About 62% stated that they were not married either by choice or stated divorce. Again, about 5% of those married stated they were separated, but for the most part no reason was given. As far as reasons for the divorce, less than 10% stated that incarceration was the cause, and one person stated that post traumatic stress syndrome led to his divorce. Unfortunately, most did not give a reason for their separation, divorce, or just not being married period.

d) Should men or women serving life sentences, or long prison sentences get married?

Approximately 71 % said yes they should if they desire to, and about 28% said no they should not. Only a handful stated they were not sure. This is a question that seems to bring much controversy, especially concerning the role of the male, due to the limited ability to serve as the husband and/or father figure while incarcerated.

e) Do you believe in God?

100% said yes to this question. It is rather foolish to think that in a population of over 3,300 inmates, with the vast mixture of people types here, that you would not have a handful of non-believers or confirmed atheists roaming around. To put it bluntly, the actions and words of some people certainly do not exhibit or display a belief in God, even though some may profess it.

f) What is your chosen faith?

Out of all surveyed, it appeared as if about 54% confess Christianity in some form, including denominations such as Methodist, Baptist, Penticostal, Episcopal, independent or non-denominational, and Catholicism. The next highest, about 44% of those surveyed, practice Islam - again with a number of different sects being encompassed under the main faith or teaching. Only about two percent listed no confessed faith, with one confessed Buddhist and one person of the Jewish faith. This survey does not reveal the fact that in this particular jail the Islamic faith outnumbers any other, with a following of about 60% or possibly more. The Christian faith has the next highest number of followers, with all others following after that. These numbers vary from jail to jail, due to location and population.

g) Do you have peace of mind?

Approximately 53% said they have peace of mind. On the other hand, about 47% stated they do not, and a couple said sometimes, with no explanation. One person even asked what our definition of "peace of mind" is. Obviously it varies greatly from person to person.

h) Were you and your spouse living together at the time of your arrest?

Approximately 65% of all surveyed said they were. Some crossed out the word spouse and wrote "girl" or "friend", so we assume that not all couples were married. About 25% said they were not living together, which again does not clarify legal spouse, common-law spouse or other arrangement. It also does not clarify separation or divorce in many cases. About 10% did not comment.

i) Did you ever serve in the military?

Approximately 39% stated they did, while about 60% stated they did not. Roughly 1% did not comment.

j) Were you ever a registered voter? If so, did you ever vote in any public election?

About 55% of all surveyed said they were registered to vote, with about 1% not commenting. Of those who were registered, about 85% stated that they did vote in a public election. About 5% did not comment as to whether they voted or not.

k) Did you ever smoke, drink, or use drugs? Are you doing one or any of these now?

Approximately 67% of all surveyed said they did have one or more of the above habits at one time, with about 31% stating they did not. Roughly 7% did not comment. About 28% said they now are engaged in one or more of the habits, with about 46% stating that they no longer are. Roughly 26% did not comment. What we do not know is if some of the users now were all users before, or if some just recently started. It does appear though that almost all users are smoking cigarettes or cigars as stated on the questionnaire. It is a known fact that mostly any controlled substance can be and is found in jails, whether it's for smoking, snorting, or injecting. No matter how candid and secret a survey is, most people would not necessarily reveal exactly what they are smoking or drinking or using in some fashion. Incidentally, in the year 1996 in this prison alone, inmates spent roughly about $343,000.00 on cigarettes. Our inmate population has been averaging about 3,300 to 3,600 men at one time, which is down considerably from around 4,000 people five or six years ago. Due to some renovating on the cell blocks and general overcrowding, every attempt is being made to keep the population around 3,300 to 3,800 inmates. When the count was up around 4,000 the cigarettes and tobacco amounts were running many thousands of dollars more than the above figure.

One interesting comment that was noted as an explanation was as follows: "I stopped using drugs because I no longer saw my mother's son in the mirror." It is unfortunate that more substance abusers do not come to this realization sooner, before it is indeed too late.

l) Do you have any health or medical problems? If the answer is yes, please list the problems.

As far as health is concerned, inmates in general are very healthy people. Many eat fairly well, stay in good shape, and of course get plenty of rest. Approximately 68% of all surveyed stated they have no known health problems. Roughly one percent did not comment, which left about 31% of all surveyed who said they had one or more health problems. It is interesting to note that things many of us in the civilian world would consider problems, inmates do not. Some of these things they have learned to live with, or just are ignorant of the impending danger or shortcoming, so they do not consider them a problem. Likewise, things that we would never think of going to the Doctor for or seeking help for, mostly for economic reasons or the infinitesimally of the problem, inmates sometimes make an issue of. This also is due to economics - due to the fact that the treatment is free. Some of the common problems noted are as follows:

1) Bad headaches.
2) Bad feet.
3) Kidney failure (in a few cases).
4) Crone's disease.
5) Arthritis.
6) Diabetes.
7) Ulcers.
8) High cholesterol.
9) High blood pressure.
10) Various skin diseases.
11) Low back pain.
12) Asthma.
13) G. I. problems - stomach, bowl, etc.
14) H.I.V./Aids.
15) Sports injuries.
16) Bad eyesight.
17) Bad knees.
18) Various social diseases.

One individual indicated a potential mental problem in his statement as follows: "I am frustrated about being here. If I don't get out soon, I'll be just as crazy as the judge that sent me here."

Another unique individual also indicated an impending problem in his statement as follows: "As a Black man in the U.S. suffering the racism of our society, I am sure I suffer from some neurosis."

There are a fair number of people in jail with chronic and some definite life threatening illnesses whether due to a lifetime of bad eating habits, substance abuse, lack of exercise, old age, bad hygiene, emotional and physical abuse, or of course - bad judges and racism - to mention a few. When incarcerating someone as punishment for a crime, one or any number of these listed above along with other possibilities may accompany the inmate to and through the system. Nevertheless, they are now the system's responsibility, and must be cared for until their release or death, whichever happens to come first.

m) Do you have a blood relative in the prison where you are housed?

About 85% stated they do not, leaving about 15% who stated they do. We do not know by this whether the relative or relatives are fellow inmates or staff. By policy, relatives who are both inmate and staff are not supposed to be located in the same institution, especially if the staff member has close inmate contact. Normal procedure is to transfer the inmate to another jail if a staff member happens to be a blood relative.

n) Do you get visits? If so, how often?

Of all people surveyed, approximately 75% said they receive visits on a fairly regular basis, while the remaining 25% stated they do not. Normally, you can have a visit for every Sunday of the month as far as number, and it can be used any day or evening of the week, provided the jail is running on normal operating status. The number of visits of those who said yes range from one time per year, usually on a family day, to 52 times per year, or one for every Sunday that comes. About one third of those getting regular visits average about three per month. The other two thirds seem to average about two to five per year. One man stated he does get visits, but only a few per year because it makes everyone feel bad. One other inmate stated he does not want any visits because he refuses to inflict his pains on his loved ones.

The last of the questions pretty much deal with life and feelings of the inmate right now in jail, and anticipated future plans. The questions are as follows:

a) At this moment as you read this, how long have you been incarcerated?

As extremes go, one man with the least amount of time out of all surveyed stated he has been in jail for one month and 30 days. The inmate with the most time in as of this survey, has 24 years and five months incarceration time. The average out of all surveyed came out to be about eight years, three months and seven days. Whether it is one century, one decade, or one day, it is a challenge that most of us do not care to try and meet.

b) Do you have a job? If not, why not? Please explain.

Of all the people surveyed, approximately 90% stated they are working at a job. Most of the remaining ten percent said they could not get a job due to transfer status or jobs not being available. It is a known fact that there are not enough jobs to go around for all who can and want to work, which is not any fault of the inmates themselves. There are a few who have had jobs, but for some reason have lost them. One man stated he lost his job due to using obscene language. Disciplinary actions usually are the main factor. One inmate even stated that he does not have a job, due to the fact that he is a certified chef with A.C.F., and refuses to be a "slave". Another stated that he just finished his G.E.D., and is now on the waiting list for a job. There should certainly be enough jobs available for all who want to work, but unfortunately this is another shortcoming of the existing system, which tends to contribute to non-productivity and potentially dangerous idle time among inmates.

c) What do you do to maintain your sanity?

Many answers to this question were very similar to the other question that was asked about survival in prison. Many of the people surveyed stated that they read and pray a lot, with a few mentioning attendance at Bible studies. A fair number said they watch television and exercise in various ways. Some mentioned attending school, working, attending meetings for various organizations and programs, and creativity such as art and music. Some of the single opinion and unique answers were as follows:

1) Observe the craziness around me and refuse to be a part of it.
2) I work, I'm in the veterans organization, I go to church, and try to get involved in any worthwhile program or group, and work to better myself, others, and all mankind.
3) Nothing but trust in God.
4) Hope.
5) Good question.
6) Take care of myself.
7) Ignore all of the fools.
8) Survive day to day and trust God.
9) I grow flowers.
10) Keep away from the nuts.
11) Laugh a lot.
12) Keep in mind that I will be released someday.
13) I keep near to God and close to my family.
14) Think of the good things that are in store for me and think positive.
15) Write.
16) Play Music.
17) Pray, Fast, Read the Word of God.
d) What is the most valuable possession you have in prison?

Approximately 40% stated that the most valuable thing they had was their own life. Immediately following that was a good mind, sound body, and family pictures (wife, kids, etc.) A few listed things such as friends, good health, books, and their Bible and Qu'ran (Koran). Some of the other items listed were as follows:

1) My trumpet and case.
2) My instruments.
3) Word processor.
4) T.V.
5) Legal papers.
6) Books.

7) Radio.
8) Legal mail.
9) Typewriter.
10) Shoes.
11) Art supplies.
12) My belief and faith in God.
13) My sanity.
14) My dignity and self-respect.
15) My soul.

Two simply stated "nothing". One individual stated very bluntly "me, myself, and I".

e) If there were a fire or flood in your cell, what is the one thing you would want to save?

This question was answered overwhelmingly with the same items, and answers as stated to the previous question. A few more stated that they would want to save themselves along with the most valuable items, in their cells, but for the most part the answers were a ditto of the previous question.

f) Who or what has helped you the most during incarceration?

Some of the varied answers were as follows:

1) My friend.
2) Nothing yet - I just got here.
3) Fellow workers.
4) My family.
5) A priest.
6) Education, solitude, religion, friends, some staff, and mainly family members.
7) Myself.
8) Other inmates, some staff, friends, family.
9) The music department, playing music, typing.
10) God.

11) Religion.

12) Bible study.

13) Working.

14) Outside clearance, working on the farm.

15) Being active and using this place as my tool for freedom.

16) Reading good books.

17) N.A. Meetings.

18) Art.

19) Islam and believing Brothers.

20) Allah.

21) Two staff doctors.

22) College programs.

23) Other inmates who cared.

24) My mother.

25) Sisters.

26) The church.

27) Family unity.

28) My spiritual values and faith thereof.

29) The education deparment.

30) Phone time (to keep in touch with relatives).

31) Allah (God) All praise be to God.

32) The law clinic.

33) Friends.

34) Nobody except my mother.

35) The Deputy Superintendent, school, and belonging to groups.

36) The Lord Jesus Christ.

g) What are your plans upon release?

1) Get out of Pennsylvania.

2) Work.

3) Work, save money, then move to a cabin in upstate PA or Alaska.

4) Take care of my son.

5) To stay out.

6) Be a drug and alcohol counselor.

7) Get close to Allah and my children.

8) Get employment and be reunited with my wife and children.
9) To continue in church and re-establish my business.
10) Go to a drug rehab.
11) Work and live peacefully.
12) Seek a holy spiritual freedom (maturity).
13) Get married.
14) Go to school.
15) Start my own business.
16) Don't know.
17) Get involved in A.A. - see psychologist and psychiatrist.
18) Support my family, mentally and physically.
19) Become an artist.
20) Get my chef's degree.
21) Go home and never set food on U.S. soil again.
22) Start a new life.
23) Pay backs.
24) Buy a house.
25) Be a better person.
26) To live as civilly, humanly and peacefully as I possibly can, and live a lifestyle that is pleasing to my Lord, and conducive to common sense.
27) With my life sentence, I do not make any plans, but first take it a day at a time. I always do the best I can and work for the good of us all.
28) Return to the communities that I once hurt, and pay for the damages done to them. Also, go to Bible school, and teach about the change God can make in a person's life.

Last but not least, I asked the inmates to tell us how they feel about everything that has happened to them from the moment of their arrest until now - including arrest, trial, conviction, sentencing, and time served. The answers were nothing less than interesting and informative. Again, due to space, I chose the ones that were unique and best summed up the majority of answers given. They are as follows:

1) I feel (as I know) I am persecuted.

2) I feel violated.
3) I am tired of this jailing - I am getting tired of doing time.
4) It was all hell and mostly unnecessary.
5) Nonsense.
6) It happened.
7) Over all bad.
8) I got illegally convicted.
9) It stinks.
10) No comment.
11) I feel I've earned this situation with my actions, but I don't like the situation I'm in.
12) I didn't feel too good coming into here, however, now I feel much better because my release date is near.
13) I was really high at the time of my crime and during sentencing. I have come a long way - I am going to college, and I am focused on what I need to do, and nothing will stop me from doing it.
14) I feel I deserved some punishment, but the police didn't have to make up evidence or lie to get a conviction. I still see people working here (prison) selling drugs, breaking laws, running books and numbers, stealing, lying, beating inmates, and are poor examples for inmates to change by. Most laws were and still are broken to keep me here.
15) Screwed with my pants on.
16) I could not answer it in any kind of brief statement.
17) I understand now, what the people (my people) in the south was going through.
18) I have been intimidated by the courts, I have been cheated by the courts, and I have been dehumanized by the prison system.
19) Since my arrest, I have gotten my GED, and also stopped using drugs. I have gained back my family. Even though I'm serving a life sentence I still feel free because now I got peace of mind.
20) From the time of my arrest until the present time, I've been through a gauntlet of different feelings.

143

21) The justice system in Pennsylvania is unfair, corrupt, political, and violates most of the U.S. Constitution. The state prison system is still in the dark ages.

22) I feel real depressed, but we can't beat the system, so I had a bad trial but I got to roll with it.

23) I feel that I have been treated unfairly by the courts, and even now in prison. Corrupt men are treated better by the courts, and by the prison. But I thank God for His strength and love.

24) I feel stupid for not learning to be a good person from my previous experiences.

25) I feel as though I should not be doing time for aggravated assault I didn't commit. I am mad as hell, that's how I feel.

26) If I was to say I was guilty, which I am not, but if we were to assume this, a life sentence here in Pennsylvania is too severe because in other states you may serve years less. A murder in Pennsylvania is more severe than in other states.

27) I knew I was sick, that is why I turned myself in. I've been through so much agony and pain I do not want to remember it. As of right now I just about forgot all of it and the bad times I had. Now things are looking real good.

28) Unfair.

29) Unpleasant, but deserved.

30) My arrest was like a nightmare. My trial was not fair because not all the facts were given. The police lied about what happened or told what they thought happened. I knew I would be convicted. At sentencing I was shocked at all the time they gave me. As far as my time there, I try and make the best of it. I do feel at times that I am wasting my time in here when I could be doing more and better things on the streets and for people who cared more for the things I do. I get angry over people not doing a good job, and their lack of responsibility, be it guards or inmates, and not have pride in their work.

31) If I can mimic the words of a great person for the lack of my own wrong..."I've been hoodwinked", I have been cheated and deprived my life through falsified evidence gleaned by the Commonwealth (District Attorney and police) to imprison me because I refused to cooperate with them and implicate other people as perpetrators of the crime I've been accused. I was arrested on 2/22/83, my trial was on December 13th through the 16th, 1983. I was sentenced to life in prison for Murder (felony) by a jury verdict on 12/16/83. To this date, I have served 13 years and 21 days of my life in prison for a crime I am innocent of.

32) Anger, shock, disillusionment, fear, acceptance, goal setting.

33) The arrest was very drastic and could have been fatal to me. Police brutality is taken for granted it if you survive. The trial was a railroad job and I pleaded guilty which was the lesser of the evils. The sentence could have been much longer had I gone to trial, and I was told I would not win. In a prison environment people are treated in a manner in which I have never seen a human being treat another in such way. A person is conditioned to be lied to and cheated in an atmosphere where there is no honor or trust, and this comes from those who are entrusted to be society's custodians. We are dogged and lied to, we are used to further the goals of those who are entrusted to prepare us to return to society and function in an arena of fairness and honesty. We are used as fools. We are conditioned to expect to be lied to and distrust authority. They get caught wrong and we pay the price. They get called on the carpet and they spend tax payers money and lock us up, and make up all kinds of new rules to cause us more suffering.

I will close this chapter by simply saying that you have just read the real thing. The comments by the inmates to the questions are just as we received them on paper. Not always grammatically correct with perfect punctuation, but just as they write and speak. As I mentioned before, I could not begin to list every response out of the hundreds received, but after reading this chapter, hopefully you the reader can appreciate the thoughts and feelings of the inmates as human beings, and not just individuals convicted of a crime.

Freedom of Choice

I am frequently asked by friends, relatives, and acquaintances, about the quality of life in jail. Inquiring minds want to know just how life is behind bars. In fact, one friend of mine who knew I was writing about jail, said that he wants to be able to read my book and be convinced from what he reads, that he would never willingly do anything to end up there. That is precisely the reason why I included this chapter. Other than the conditions already mentioned about the prison environment, here are some things to seriously think about and consider before knowingly and willingly doing something to cause yourself to be able to call prison your home.

Many people feel that inmates have too much, too many privileges, and too little responsibility in paying back their debt to society. Much of society feels that television and cable should not be permitted in jail, even though inmates pay for both if they choose to have them. Many people are of the opinion that jail is too soft, too much like home, and that the average inmate has it better in jail than on the street. Well, this may be true if one is homeless or in a destitute way with nothing and nobody, but as I consider myself an average citizen with an average income; I, and in my worst nightmare, could not imagine jail to be an average or anywhere near average way of life, nor do many inmates - even though on the surface they appear to fit into the jail lifestyle without much difficulty.

In reality, the average person does not, or for that matter cannot, even imagine and realize what they are giving up and will be limited to when coming to jail. Whether it would be a deterrent even if they did know and realize it is uncertain, since most people committing crimes are not taking even a moment to think of the consequences of their actions. It obviously is not a deterrent to many who have served time before and returned, as evidenced by the growing number of parole violators who do not demonstrate the responsibility it takes to stay out, or the ones' who have served time previously and returned with a new sentence.

Regardless of that fact, when one becomes incarcerated, there are many things that are beyond one's control. The privilege of choice in many situations is no longer a privilege. For example, one cannot choose the type of water he drinks, for there is only one type. One may not order certain foods of his liking done in a certain way, for there is only one menu, done one way. One may not choose the type of mattress he sleeps on, because there is only one type of mattress - usually very thin and with no support - if one gets a mattress. One does not have the option of always taking a nice private shower or bath with the water at just the right temperature -for some days it's hot, some days it's cold, and for various reasons, it might not happen at all on a certain day. If one does indeed have the privilege of getting some sort of shower on a certain day, it still can only be taken at certain times of the day. By the way, it is not uncommon to be in there with strangers whose motives may not be the purist, so one must always be alert and on guard while in the steamy environment.

Once incarcerated, one must even give up the privilege of fluffing their pillow and getting it just right, as they snuggle into that certain position most desirable to begin the sleep cycle. Why? Because the pillows are so thin, they do not fluff well, if at all - and secondly, a pillow to many is a privilege, especially those who just arrived. The same goes for blankets by the way, even in the dead of winter.

If that is not enough to make you think twice about coming to jail, here's more. One who is incarcerated does not have their choice of a Doctor, Dentist, Specialist, hospital, or second opinion from another Doctor of their choice if they did not like the first (and many times only) opinion. The choice of generic or brand medication and the friendly face of a pharmacist does not exist. In fact, it could be hours or days until you even see so much as a tylenol. The option of giving your Doctor a quick call to find out some test results or get advice is not an option in jail. Even getting out of your cell during lock up time when in severe pain or needing immediate medical attention, can and has been an impossibility at times. Dialing the nearest ambulance, emergency room, or the ever popular "911", is no longer a choice one can or will have to make once incarcerated.

All of us know what it is like when the flu bug or virus hits. When that vomiting and diarrhea starts, all we want to do is to be left alone to deal with that situation from hell. If you are anything like me; as crude as it sounds, I just want to heave and expel in privacy. No audience, no conversation, and no waiting to use the facilities. Well folks, not so in jail.

Unless you are one of the very few and very fortunate anymore to have a cell to yourself - and they are getting to be fewer and fewer due to prison overcrowding - you are right there locked in the same little room with that flu bug, its' victim, and all its nasty side effects. Even if you are fortunate enough to get out for a few hours during the day, guess what's waiting for you when you return? (provided you are not the one who actually has the bug - yet.) You are right there to hear it, see it, smell it, and be exposed to it. The moaning, groaning, and all of the other unpleasantries associated with an illness such as this, not to mention any bad hygiene practices if they exist also - are all yours to share with your cellmate, or "celly" as you are commonly known. Just another reality of jail life folks.

As crappy as jail life is, it may become even more so when one runs out of toilet paper and is told to wait until tomorrow to get some - especially in the situation just described. You better know someone who is willing to give some up at that point. Toilet paper, soap, and other precious items vital to ones' personal hygiene, are only distributed on certain days during the month or depending on what it is, must be obtained at commissary on a certain day of the week. There are no convenience stores to hop in the car and go to, and of course no cars either.

How many of us are used to air conditioning during the hot summer time? How about a comfortably heated room or house during the cold winter months? Climate control is a big luxury that one misses when coming to jail. As mentioned in the introduction, there are no thermostats on the wall of the cell. Whatever temperature it is, so be it. Try to imagine yourself lying in a small cell that can easily get to be 100 degrees or more, with no fan and in some cases, windows that do not open. Or during the winter months, feeling numb in bed with a thin sheet over you, and if you are lucky, a blanket. I've seen cells in the older area of the jail, that even with the heater turned on (which is located next to the ceiling by the way), have window sills that can be used for refrigerators, due to the ice that forms on the windows - inside. This is not my idea of the comfort zone.

Even in my office, where there is a thermostat, it usually is cold in the winter, warm in the summer, or extremely cold all year around. Whether the dial is set on 50 degrees or 90 degrees, the temperature usually remains about the same. If it gets extremely cold, I can always put my pre-cut customized pieces of cardboard up in the vents, which eventually helps to raise the temperature to a somewhat habitable level. Even for employees, the option of a comfortable working climate is not an option many times. Need to hear more? Alright.

How many times does a security team come barging into your house or dwelling place in society and tear apart your belongings, keeping anything they think you should not have? (We're talking here in the U.S.A.) Have you had your television or radio opened up lately in the search for illegal weapons or drugs? Have you had any shelves torn off of your walls or personal pictures destroyed? Have you had any items deemed legal to possess and fully paid for, removed and lost forever without a refund or even a record of confiscation?

Have you had anyone force your door open lately and demand sex (particularly if they are the same sex as you are), or money, or other assets - or suffer the consequences if you do not comply? When was the last time someone in authority yanked your curtains down and shinned a light in your face while you were sleeping, just to see if you were there? Or, when was the last time you were told to go into your house, you were locked in involuntarily, and had no idea when you would be released just because some people at the other end of the street were fighting?

Well, I think you get the picture. Without giving any more examples, one can easily understand that these real life common practices in prison are not most peoples' idea of a pleasant lifestyle. The simple, everyday needs and desires that are met by running to the store, opening the refrigerator, turning on the faucet, or even walking out of the house at will are many times a rarity and a privilege, and some of the niceties many of us enjoy are never again an option when becoming incarcerated.

Beyond all of the material needs and luxuries that we in this society are so accustomed to in making life a little easier and more pleasant, there is a function and a need to be met emotionally and psychologically. Since most of us have at least one or more relatives alive somewhere in society, the exchange and meeting of these needs is important to our existence on a daily basis. Once one becomes incarcerated, the ability to share and meet these needs and experiences is greatly hindered. For most of us, the phone is a very vital link in our relationships, business deals, and meeting certain needs and desires. Once incarcerated, the phone is a limited access privilege, and must be shared by hundreds or thousands of others also. Who you may call is limited, and so is talk time. I've seen people who were stabbed because they talked an extra minute or two over their time, thus cutting into the already limited time of the next inmate waiting to make a call. One phone on a cell block - used by dozens or hundreds of inmates - can and is a vital link between sanity and insanity, and may help make the difference between marriage and divorce, success and failure, or even life and death. A tool and a luxury that some people have a few of in their homes, one in the car, boat, or even their pocket - but rarely stop to imagine how life would be without them, or at best -very limited access to one.

The option of writing letters or sending homemade cards is one that is experienced frequently in jail. For those who can write, a vital link with family and friends can be maintained even if the phone is not used. This is often not so with those who are illiterate. Some will pay other inmates to write letters for them, but again in jail, everything has its price. The best option for these individuals is to get an education, so their dependency upon others could become less.

The choice of attending a childs or grandchilds sports event, music recital, school play or graduation, is of course no longer an option. Attending a loved ones wedding, or baby shower, or anniversary party is now no more than a desire and a dream once one becomes incarcerated. One can only envision themselves in attendance and celebrating the occasion, but the four walls of the prison cell can quickly terminate the festivities and be a larger than life reminder of life as they now know it.

Just beyond the emotional happiness of occasions celebrated as progressive steps on the ladder of life, the psychologically and emotionally draining reality of death is ever present while incarcerated. One of the most difficult situations for one to have to deal with while incarcerated is the loss of a loved one. Death in itself is viewed by many as the ultimate separation from those most cherished and loved. Depending on how one may view the physical finality of that moment, certainly can determine the emotional and psychological continuance of anyone left behind.

In the prison population, emotions are already at a stressed level, and many inmates psychologically are unstable to begin with. Some base all they know to be real and true on what they can see and touch. Without any comprehension or belief in the separation of body and spirit, the physical death of a loved one may certainly seem like the end. For those who view life as a never ending journey - comprehending and believing in the separation of the physical body from the spirit at the moment of physical death - the impact and the sting that the news of death brings is many times easier to deal with.

Nonetheless, the most difficult aspect of dealing with the death of a loved one while incarcerated is not one of a spiritual void, but rather a physical separation due to incarceration. Believe it or not, just not being able to be there - at the hospital, at the house, at the funeral home, at the gravesite - is for the most part, the worst. One who is incarcerated feels quite helpless in this situation, due to the inability to comfort family, friends, and by the same token, be comforted themselves. The inability to assist in making funeral arrangements and taking care of necessary details for the days ahead leaves many saddled with the feeling of not being able to bear the burden and do their part.

News of this sort usually reaches the inmate by one of two ways - word of mouth from someone who has been in touch with the family, or through the office of the Chaplain. When an inmate receives an unexpected pass to report to the Chapel, he usually tries to prepare himself for the worst. Most, if not all inmates, know that a pass to see the chaplain on the spur of the moment usually brings bad news. The system is set up so that the chaplain, and appropriately so - is the one delegated to deliver news of a death, sudden illness, or tragedy. Unless the inmate finds out through word of mouth and calls home first, the unexpected chapel pass usually means only one thing - bad news.

In the case of a family death, an inmate does have the option at times of actually attending the viewing or the funeral. This is at the inmate's expense. Payment for the sheriffs to escort an inmate to and from the service is solely the inmates responsibility. Once arriving at the service, the inmate is escorted into the building in handcuffs and leg irons, sometimes through a different entrance than everyone else, and many times before or after everyone else has come and gone. Family contact is minimal if it occurs at all, due to security reasons.

Many inmates choose not to attend the service due to cost and the manner in which they are treated while there. Some feel it is too demeaning to be marched into the building at such a somber occasion with shackles on and led by armed guards. They feel that it is enough trauma for the family to deal with, without seeing them in such a restricted state.

Inmates in general feel the impact of death more so due to restriction and such a limitation in being able to help and just be there. Not being able to help make arrangements, pay for costs, and just console other family and friends is many times the most frustrating part of the whole ordeal. And of course, in the days, weeks, months, and years to come following the death - especially if it was a parent, spouse, or child - the constant reminiscing and thoughts of "how it could have been" or "what could have been done if only I were not locked up" can be very agonizing and painful for a long time to come.

In essence, there is really not much to be said for the conditions under which incarcerated people live, other than most people do not, and would not want to live that way. The fact that

153

jail life is a step up for some, is an indication of what life must have been like on the street. The fact that it is quite a step down for others, should be an incentive to obey the law and do what it takes to stay out - if and when they leave. The fact that so many return over and over again with violations and new sentences says a lot about their home lives and their lack of responsibility-to themselves and to others.

Whether the crime was committed as a result of spontaneity, greed, revenge, anger, rage, ignorance, peer pressure, mental disorder, or mere desperation, does not change the fact that a crime was committed. The real fact now is, that the convict will be going to a not-so-nice place to live while paying their debt to society. The fact that inmates seem to do well there or appear to have it pretty easy still does not mean that it is a nice place to live. It merely indicates that people can adapt to anything if they have to. It could indicate, if anything, that the corrections system may need to be structured differently and operated in a way so as to create an environment that would be more of a deterrent and less of an invitation for people of non-conformity and reckless living - with the exception of a few.

In short, prison is one condition of life, where good living is definitely not an option.

Food For Thought

The subject of prisons and prisoners seems to have a way of stimulating conversation and opening discussion. The discussions then seem to always cultivate new thoughts and ideas on how to deal with this element of society that is now fighting to dominate local and state budgets throughout the country. The subject of crime and recidivism has a multi-billion dollar price tag attached to it and, as mentioned earlier, is one of the biggest businesses in existence today. Taxpayers are torn between not wanting their dollars going to make convicted criminals comfortable, but yet anxious to see the criminals off the streets and out of society at all costs. The only problem is, it takes mucho bucks to accomplish this and maintain it.

Most people coming to jail are not anxious to be there, and do find it somewhat uncomfortable. This varies with each inmate. Whether it be the threat of danger, the food, the confinement, or any other limitations, there is usually something that is undesirable about it to most, if not all inmates. This leads us to the discussion involving recidivism.

One can never fully appreciate the conditions of jail unless they have been there. All the stories in the world can only halfway simulate the actual address change so to say. So, in all fairness, you could not really base the entry and preconception of one into the system for the first time, on the same standard as one with a working knowledge of the system previously. I think it is easier to understand someone coming to jail for the first time with no previous criminal history, than it is a repeat offender who is fully aware of the environment they so greatly despise coming back to.

No one ever said jail was to be nice, comfortable, or allow easy access to luxuries enjoyed by free society. Should inmates then be permitted to have access to televisions, radios, magazines, newspapers, unlimited outside phone calls (within the time frame permitted to each inmate), or even cable T.V. that they themselves pay for? Do you think that these attainable items provide positive input for the prison environment, or do you think they are more of a distraction to inmates, so the thoughts of doing bad things are hopefully kept at a minimum? Do you think if an inmate can sit in his or her cell and watch TV., listen to the radio, or read, that they would be less likely to think about escaping or getting involved in other mischief?

Beyond all that, do you think it is a factor in so many people returning to jail, knowing that they can, and do, have some or all of the comforts of home, (depending on where they lived) despite the confinement?

Some agree that if it were much more difficult to gain access to these "luxury items" in jail, that some people would think twice about doing whatever they do, or don't do, to be brought back. Whether it is taking more responsibility to follow parole guidelines, or seeking help to stop a drug or alcohol habit which can result in a crime to feed that habit, or even change a desire or lust for some material thing that can only be obtained through dishonest or criminal means, they tend to agree that if jail were tougher it would not be as full. Some feel that if it was just so terrible coming back - as in no T.V., Radio, Sports (other than legal yard time), 23 hour a day lock-up, even limited conversation - that many would conform more to the rules of parole and society. I even heard a theory one time that jail should return to conditions such as 40 or 50 years ago where you had a toilet, sink, bed and a Bible (of your chosen faith), and jail time was used to make serious review of your crime or violation, and get right with the Creator. I've even talked with older inmates who began their incarceration time that way. No talking at mealtime, marching single file to and from chow and work, and so on.

Corrections Officials and experts seem to think that the evolution to the present system as it is was a good and needed one, and progress has been made. But if this is so, with the more compromising state of incarceration as it is, why do more and more people mind coming to jail less and less? They say it is terrible, but why are they not taking the responsibility that is needed to stay out? How about government and economy? Would we stand a better chance of seeing less people come to jail, if more jobs were available, especially to those wearing the label of ex-con? Or, would irresponsibility and lack of discipline and desire to be law abiding, productive citizens still prevail? Could it just be the fact that it is a terrible place to end up, but that mankind in general is getting better at making the best of a bad situation?

Now, after presenting all of these questions and opinions on the subject, I will leave you with one last thought. Though appearing as somewhat symmetrical, this may make a strong statement as to why people continue to come back to jail, even after experiencing its plentiful lack of prosperous living and positive input.

Approximately 98% of all inmates returning to jail - give or take one or two percent - do not purposely do something to try and come back, or be brought back, to put it more properly. But - at the same time, they do not purposely do everything in their power to avoid it either. Countless inmates I have talked to are quick to make the statement "Hey, I didn't ask to come back." Very true. Verbally, they actually did not ask to come back, or desire as much. But, as actions speak louder than words, obviously so do law officials and their policies speak louder than forgetfulness, irresponsibility, or the diminishing desire to adhere to the rules of freedom. Think about it.

The subject that I am about to throw out to you now to stimulate your thought process is probably the most controversial one of the whole Corrections system. I tend to view it as sort of the "abortion issue" of sentencing and punishment. In fact, there are people who would never consider an abortion in a million years, but would be first in line to impose and carry out the penalty. And then there are those, who would think nothing of terminating that tiny fetal heartbeat for reasons less than logical, but could never even entertain the thought of extinguishing one's life out of payment or revenge for another.

You probably guessed it. The Death Penalty. The final end to a final end. The methodical practice of ending one's life because they ended someone else's. Let's look at some facts and statements surrounding this issue.

First of all, depending on who you are, and your relationship with the convicted party, your views will differ accordingly on the subject. If you have a son or daughter, or any other close relative that you love dearly who is sitting on death row waiting to be executed, you probably would be very much opposed to it. Many hundreds and thousands of families down through the years have emotionally plead to juries and judges to spare their loved one of that horrible demise. "Please, please I beg of you, anything but that" - "have a heart, have a conscience" - "don't take him (or her) from us, please!" There is a certain sound of finality that a death sentence carries with it, unlike any other. Likewise, if you have been the victim of a violent crime, or have lost a loved one because of such an act, pulling the switch, or trigger, or squeezing the plunger of a syringe could become second nature, and carry sweet revenge into personal satisfaction in knowing that "they got what they deserved."

Many people feel that the death penalty in all its finality would be much more of a deterrent if used on a regular basis, say weekly or monthly. They feel that if criminal minded people saw this in action for sure, they would think twice about killing someone. If they knew beyond the shadow of a doubt, that if convicted of a brutal murder or senseless killing they would also be killed as the penalty, they would think hard before committing the act. Well, it might sound good in theory, but in reality, it's questionable.

If you remember in Chapter 6 with the survey, where the inmates expressed their views, this very question appeared also. The inmates said themselves, that most thought that the death penalty is not a deterrent to crime in general, and would not be, even if regularly enforced. It is a known fact that many violent crimes occur as a spontaneous act, and not a pre-meditative process. Yes, there are those that are plotted, planned, and carried out with future plans in mind. But, what about the bank robbery, when someone makes a quick move and the gunman mistakes it as something it's not, and pulls the trigger? Or the over stressed police officer that comes home and finds his or her mate entwined with someone else, and out of sheer momentary emotional breakdown pulls their gun and kills one or both parties in the compromising position? Or, how about the mentally ill subject who may have a certain fixation or desire and at some point just "snaps", and takes one or more people out during the rage?

Domestic problems seem to be famous for these kinds of momentary, spontaneous acts of violence. Crimes of passion and jealousy are ever popular in our society today. Homicides occurring during bank robberies and burglaries, especially foiled ones, also are many times unintended, but just "happen" (to quote some inmates). Homicides as a result of sex crimes or sex fantasies running amuck are becoming more common. And of course, there are the mentally distraught or just outright mentally ill, who make a game of killing, or get a pleasure out of it somehow even into dismemberment or cannibalism, or both.

Are all of these scenarios worthy of execution? Are some but not others? Is a homicide only brutal in some cases and not others? Are there such things as justifiable homicides, or are all of them worthy of the death penalty? Who would be capable of making the decision in these cases, if a homicide was automatically an execution case? Who could ever fairly say whether one case should be exempt, or another should be pardoned, or another should definitely "fry"? (society slang) Are any of us as humans a totally fair evaluator of such acts? Most religions for example, take a certain stand or have writings within their particular Holy Book that they use, that speak for or against the subject of capital punishment - taking a life for a life for purpose of punishment for crime.

Let us look briefly at three of these religions that include the most inmates throughout the entire State Correctional System of Pennsylvania. The two largest, Christianity and Islam, both with numbers into the many thousands according to D.O.C. statistics, far exceed any other religious following by number, with those of the Jewish faith coming next - but with less than 200 incarcerated statewide.

In the Islamic faith for example, the Quran is the Holy Book and it does in fact make a statement concerning this subject. It speaks of this, according to the writings in Surah (Chapter) AL Baqara (2), Verse 178, referring to the "AL Qisaas" - or, as the Arabic term is translated, "the law of equality and punishment".

It allows for the payment and/or life of the guilty party to either be spared or taken.

According to one Imam (religious leader) that supplied me with some of this information, the works found in Surah AL Baqara (2), verse 178 stating ... "the free for the free, the slave for the slave, and the female for the female ... "mean that the specific person or persons is responsible for what he or she has done, and his or her blood for it is lawful. He stated that the AL Qisaass allows the aggrieved to seek the life of the killer of their kin, or to forgo that option and demand blood money (Ad-Diyah), if such an offer is made. (Ad-Diyah is payment for the life that was taken.) If that is the case, the killer is admonished to pay the Diyah handsomely, and with gratitude (to Allah), that his or her life was spared.

He went on to say that "equality in punishment" as it is referred to, includes in its meaning that all murderers are equally punished for their offense. In many instances, a person from among the rich or "upper class" may receive a different kind of justice than one from the poor or "lower class". The affluent people many times were given preferential treatment. Allah's decree of AL Qisaas rules out specialized justice.

According to another Iman I spoke to, there are writings known as the Al Hudud, that prescribe different punishments by Allah and/or his messenger Mohammed for crimes that are committed, and in turn are carried out by the Islamic state, rather than the aggrieved individuals themselves. He stated that there are situations where the accused party or subject has indeed been found guilty of the crime of murder, and in this case, capital punishment is indeed the prescribed sentence.

One of these religious leaders who provided me with this information offered his personal opinion on the subject - to which we are all entitled - stating his belief that "the murderer - one who has intentionally killed without cause - should pay with his or her life. While it is true that the victim of the murderer cannot be brought back to life, by the same token the killer would not be able to kill again. I believe that the removal from the face of the earth of that kind of mind is necessary and just."

By contrast, the Christian faith - including Protestants,

Catholics, and Independent Bible believers of all faiths and denominations - makes statements about this subject in its' Holy Book, the Holy Bible. In fact, the earliest record of capital punishment appears in the first book - Genesis - Chapter 9, verse 6. It states, "Whoever sheds the blood of man, by man shall his blood be shed; for in the image of God has God made man. This should not be confused with the first recorded case of murder in the Bible - in Genesis Chapter 4 - where Cain killed his brother Abel. It is interesting to note that God did not kill Cain for this act, but according to scripture, sent him away as a homeless wanderer and put a mark on him warning everyone not to kill him, or seven lives would be taken in revenge for his.

If you then move into the next book following Genesis, it is Exodus, that has several verses concerning laws about violent acts.

Beginning in Exodus 21, verse 12, then moving down through verse 23, it discusses penalties for certain acts, including the "eye for an eye, tooth for a tooth" theory. Just after Exodus, in the Book of Leviticus, Chapters 20, 24, and 26 all talk about penalties and punishment for disobedience along with examples of just and fair punishment. More examples such as these appear throughout the rest of the Old Testament and do include the penalty of death for acts such as adultery, homosexuality, and murder.

As you then read on into the New Testament, laws and ideas on punishment change somewhat with the coming of Jesus, as a message of love, mercy and forgiveness through repentance was being preached. In fact, according to scripture, Jesus himself said in Matthew 5 verse 17 in the New Testament that "I come not to abolish the law, but to fulfill it". A good illustration of this is given in the Gospel of John in the New Testament -Chapter 8, verses 3 thru 11 - referring to the woman caught in the act of adultery.

This example and others like it throughout the New Testament did not negate the fact that there still would be consequences when these laws were, or are violated, but the harsh punishment handed down for violating the Ten Commandments and laws of society in some cases was escaped or softened through the message of repentance and forgiveness for any who would wish to embrace it.

If you then look at some of the laws and writings of the Jewish faith, some similarities exist to the two previously mentioned. In theory, Jewish law requires the death penalty for certain crimes. In fact, the Jewish Bible, or Torah, justifies execution for 15 different infractions. Things such as working on Yom Kipper, blasphemy, and adultery are among those listed. The book of Leviticus, Chapter 24 verse 21, states " he that killeth a man shall be put to death". According to Rabbi Bernard Rothman, religious leader of Congregation Sons of Israel in Cherry Hill, "the Torah speaks about the death penalty in many cases - but because of the complexity, the death penalty was rarely given. "(taken from an article on the death penalty published in the Jewish exponent on April 21, 1995). In the same article, it states that "Jewish law decreed that a sentence of capital punishment required that the murder had to have been observed by two witnesses, and the witnesses had to warn the murderer that his action was punishable by death. No circumstantial evidence was accepted in capital cases."

Many Rabbis tend to take a stand against the Death penalty, as do some church leaders of other faiths, due to the inequity of its issuance. It tends to discriminate against the poor, the minorities, and the uneducated, more than any other group. The inequity seen in sentencing people to be executed along with the fact that by proof of time and statistic it is not a deterrent, is the major problem with it being recognized as just or fair punishment. The Jewish community as individuals is probably as divided on the subject of capital punishment as any other community of a certain faith, but on the whole, the death penalty tends to go against their traditions and values as Jewish people.

Regardless of what religious faith or belief one identifies with, most if not all believe that for a crime such as murder, a penalty of some severe sort should in most, if not all cases be imposed, being based on all of the circumstances of and surrounding the crime. One could seriously doubt if, in this day and time, the "eye for an eye" principle could or would be stretched to incorporate the justification of one homicide for another, or "body for body" in all cases, for purpose of punishment - or on the other hand, the pardoning of such an act upon receipt of a statement of remorse and repentance.

Other than the death penalty, life sentences with no parole are the next option, or extremely long sentences which incarcerate one into their elderly years. As an option for cases that would require a penalty of lesser degree but still somewhat severe, life sentences with parole consideration after a stipulated time period are probably the next best possibility.

Nevertheless, I think we all realize and agree that if some severe penalty is not imposed for violent criminal acts, to continue to send out a message to society that these acts are not acceptable, even though at times unintentional, society itself would be absolute chaos. Law and order must be maintained for society to survive and function. Just think - what if the penalty of death was still being carried out for one who hits their father or mother, or for kidnapping, or for the all too common act of adultery? I would venture to say that many of us would be seeing friends, relatives, neighbors, and acquaintances disappearing daily (especially for the latter of the three!).

Regardless, there seems to be many who still place a large question mark over the justification of execution as penalty and punishment, no matter how severe the crime. Some feel that if there is indeed no doubt of guilt, as in witnessing the crime in action, or totally overwhelming evidence to prove the guilty party is indeed guilty, then execution is justified. Some feel it is justified only in certain types of cases involving children and woman, namely sex and sex related homicide cases. Some feel that it is a deterrent due to the fact that the executed party absolutely will never kill again. (Or do anything else again for that matter.) And then there are those who take a stand against it totally. Others unfortunately, out of sheer ignorance and lack of knowledge and integrity, would choose to "fry em' all" (society slang) if given the opportunity. As we have all seen by statistics, "frying" anyone at any time has never even placed a dent in the torpedo of crime moving steadily through and against our society.

Interestingly enough, this was proven even more so during

the middle ages when capital punishment was being routinely practiced. During this period in history, execution increased, and so did the cruel ways of carrying it out. In the 15th century, the burning of witches at the stake was common, and carried right into the 18th Century. By contrast during the time of the Roman Empire, capital punishment was rare, and mainly used for military crimes. The Romans looked at execution as a deterrent, so they carried it out publicly - by way of burning, crucifixion, and even decapitation - hoping to send out a clear message to all who witnessed it. But to no avail, violent crimes still occurred, and still do today more than ever. No matter how violent or gruesome the punishment, acts of violent crime have never ceased.

In conclusion, no matter what religion a person identifies with, if they do at all, the opinions on the subject of Capital punishment - who, how, against, always, never... - are as numerous, and personal, and justified, as the population itself.

Your opinion is indeed - your opinion.

Now, taking all of this into consideration, we could ask ourselves the following:

a. Do we really feel justified in taking a life for a life as punishment, or is it in reality more of a sense of "revenge"?

b. If punishment is indeed the motive for execution, do we really think a procedure that takes a few moments to end a life is punishment - especially where the family and friends of the deceased will spend not minutes, but an entire lifetime living with that void?

c. Would it not be more punishment oriented to allow the convicted criminal to live, but be sentenced to hard labor and the responsibility of growing their own food (if they desire to eat), making clothes (if they desire to be clothed), building shelter (if they desire a place to get in out of the elements), and giving up all of the comforts and privileges like family, a mate, television, radio, and most other luxuries enjoyed by our society?

d. Would it not make more sense to have someone who

would have been executed (after many years of costing the tax payers two or three times the normal amount of money to keep an inmate), be self supporting and productive, instead of a total non-productive burden on the system and society - only to eventually be marched off and killed anyway, with no return or reconciliation?

e. Would we not see more of a punishment, and revenge (if so desired by certain individuals), by isolating an individual into self-sustainment for the rest of their naturals lives?

f. If execution was practiced on a consistent basis, should it be used only in the cases where the killer confessed to the crime, posted no opposition to the execution, or was identified in a way that left no doubt as to their guilt?

g. What about cases where the killer now professes to be a changed person, and displays a totally different personality and actions than at the time of the killing?

h. Would it be more advantageous to then commute their sentence to life without parole for example, so that by their example of words and actions, others could be influenced in the right direction?

i. Who could be a totally fair judge of the legitimacy of that professed change? What human being or group of human beings, is totally capable of granting mercy where mercy is due, and never allowing bias or prejudice of any degree to interfere with that decision?

j. By the same token, what if we did execute on a regular basis, but began finding out years down the road that some of the people we killed were the wrong ones? (it has happened)

k. How would you feel as the executioner?

I. How would you feel as the Judge or jury that issued the sentence?

m. How would you feel as the Governor that refused to grant the stay of execution? (Especially due to political pressure or gain.)

n. How would you feel as one who just wanted them killed because of their color or religion?

These are questions we must all ask ourselves in true honesty and sincerity when rendering opinions on the death penalty. We must always take into consideration that many deaths were not intentional, as the act of execution certainly is. We must never forget that a pre-meditated murder is totally different than a non-intentional one. We must think about cases where person "A" meant to hurt person "B", but certainly not to kill them. Or, what about cases where person "A" was under the influence of a controlled substance trying to deal with life and its' complexities, and acted totally out of character, accidentally killing someone? What about self protection - who draws the line as to whether person "A" needed to kill person "B" to stop them, or just shoot them in an arm or leg? What about domestic situations, where emotions and actions speak louder than common sense and rational thinking? How about abortions - are they pre-meditated murders? If so, why isn't that punishable by death?

The subject of the death penalty for the most part is a very personal issue. As difficult as it is to legislate morality, as in the subject of abortion, so it is as difficult for the most part to legislate the act of execution for purpose of punishment. From the political viewpoint, it makes a good issue to win votes, or for anti-crime platforms. From a victim of crime or loss of loved one standpoint, it may at times look like the answer to sweet revenge, or to be politically correct, "justice". From an understanding and compassionate parents or loved one's view (or the side of the perpetrator) it is very cruel and just not quite justified, even though some form of punishment is.

So, who decides? Who condemns? Who pardons? Where is the line of fairness and equity drawn? Besides, is everyone who is condemned to die really guilty?

I think the best way not to kill someone while driving under the influence of alcohol is to not drink and drive. There is no way it can happen if you do not drink and then drive. I think the best way to be sure that you will never die from a drug overdose caused by the voluntary use of a controlled substance, is to stop using or not use drugs period. Most likely, the best way to be sure that someone who is innocent was never or will never be put to death as an act of punishment, is to not execute at all in the name of justice. Most likely, there are much better ways of incurring punishment within the humane realm, with the added possibility of being able to reverse a decision or sentence later in time, if proof of innocence presents itself - not so, with one already executed.

Think about it.

Rehabilitation - Brains vs. Bodies

Re-ha-bil-i-tate\, [rē (h)ə-'bil-ətāt')
1. To restore (a handicapped or delinquent person) to useful life through education and therapy. 2. To reinstate the good name of. 3. To restore the former rank, privileges, or rights of.

Is the system restoring inmates to useful life through education and therapy? Is it reinstating the good name of people who became incarcerated? Is it restoring the former rank, privileges, and rights of inmates through incarceration?

Hardly. In fact, the corrections system in terms of distance, is probably light years away in achieving all the conditions mentioned in the definition of rehabilitation. It is obvious by now that we have more than met the criteria for locking people away, in fact we do it so well that we cannot build prisons fast enough to accommodate the rapid influx. Unfortunately, a significant percentage of this return crowd has visited here before, only to return again - and some again, and again. In fact, I know of one inmate who is back for the fourth time in approximately three years on parole violations. I know of a few others who have come and gone three or four times, each time with a new sentence for a variety of different crimes. This track record certainly does not fit the description of rehabilitation. To many of us, it would better fit the category of dehumanization.

Many who work in the realm of corrections consider the jail environment sub-human in reality. To literally strip you of your clothes, jewelry, possessions, and dignity, certainly is not the way most of us would choose or desire to live. The discouraging side to this is that many of the systems returnees appear as if they are not really bothered or devastated about returning. In fact, once they get off the bus, or whatever they arrived in, smiles and laughter seem to abound. For some, it's like old home week. We see all inmates the following working day after they have arrived, and many times observe looks of fear, sadness, disgust and/or frustration - but an attitude of contentment, and even fun and games accompany some. This of course could be, and is in reality a front, but certainly not in all cases. Within hours, some inmates have in their possession or access to cigarettes, commissary, drugs, or even weapons. Joking, laughing, greeting old acquaintances, friends or relatives, and just fitting back into the flow seems to be the issue at hand. The fact that their fragile lives, with whatever positive assets and attributes they may contain, have just been plucked from society and demeaned once again, seems to have little impact on their ego or outlook in general. Sadly enough, for those whose lives have been a constant downhill journey and uphill struggle, this environment actually is a pleasant plateau for the time being.

When analyzing the subject of recidivism and rehabilitation, we must first understand the inmates themselves and some characteristics common to their nature.

For the most part, inmates are thinking people. Unfortunately, many are usually thinking about the wrong things and the wrong way of operating in society, rather than conforming to the rules and standards that people are expected to follow. In many cases, they appear to have been attempting to attain things, both wanted and needed in life, in a way that is unacceptable according to societies rules - basically illegally, immorally, and underhandedly. In some cases it is evident, that their whole goal for the hours that they are awake, night or day, is to undermine and circumvent the system. Then, when they are arrested and convicted, they cry injustice and unfair practice on the part of the law and society. This practice of cheating, lying, and deception many times reflects in their jail life, only to perpetuate and spawn new problems within this already problem burdened society of the incarcerated.

To most inmates, there is a logic to and behind everything they do, even though it may be illogical or illegal by most or all standards. Unfortunately, the same standards they lived by that sent them to prison, they continue to use to live life while incarcerated, and in many cases return to the street with - only to repeat the cycle once again. It should be understood that those standards and methods of operation used by these inmates mentioned, have been adopted and used for many years, and are only a manifestation of character and personality observed and pictured at an early age. A child is not born knowing how to steal, lie, cheat, or be corrupt in any way. These are learned traits, and who better to learn them from than a parent, family member, or friend. This fact, together with environment and poor support systems in the community, all help to contribute to the reasoning behind the actions of many inmates. This is precisely why the number of parole violators has risen and is continuing to rise at an alarming rate. These individuals for the most part have not changed their way of life or standards by which they live, but feel they must work around the system instead of working with it.

It should be understood, that many inmates operate this way either due to the way they grew up, or their conditioning while incarcerated, or of course both. The combination of both is not uncommon to many. Due to the many authority figures they encounter and must deal with throughout the prison system, not to mention previous scars left by childhood, early adolescence, law officers, etc., they have found and continue to find ways of working around the so called "obstacles" that they see as restrictions. By the time many inmates are of age to enter the state prison system, the word "no" is more than common verbiage. The idea of not being able to express one's opinion or need, and being told no repeatedly upon request of something, is as common as breathing in many cases. The individual has conditioned his or herself to the fact, and now reacts accordingly. As unlawfully or violatory as it may be, their method of operating has worked for them in the past so they continue to practice it. As previously mentioned, most parole violators do not return with new charges or cases, but rather minor infractions or technical violations (commonly called "techs"). These technical violations, as minor as they may seem, are a direct result of the still present rebellion, irresponsibility and lawless attitude that controls their lives for the most part. In all fairness, as mentioned before, it is very easy and at times convenient for a spouse or other party to call the parole officer and issue a complaint, which will many times bring the parolee back to jail. But, the returns with the confirmed non-valid complaints are usually few. For the most part, they have been read and

171

instructed on the conditions of parole, but many still choose to do things the way they would rather do them. This does not say they are bad people, but their attitude towards authority is obviously way out of line, and they are not taking the responsibilities necessary to retain their freedom. Then, when returning to prison on a ridiculous technicality, the system is unjust by their measurement.

I can recall not long ago, having two parole violators on the same morning - in fact, one right after the other - tell me they were returned to jail for driving without a license. One happened to be doing very well at a halfway house, and in fact had been driving for some time without a license. After being stopped for a traffic violation, he was discovered. To him it was no big deal, since "a lot of people do it" as he stated.

The other inmate happened to open the conversation by asking me, "Did you ever have a rude awakening?" to which I replied "yes, a few times in my life!" I did not know what he was getting at in the beginning, so I questioned him further. He proceeded to tell me that he was "nabbed" yesterday in a phone booth by his parole officer, and told that he was going back to prison for driving without a license. He stated that he woke up this morning in the cell and thought, "now how could this happen?" (referring to the rude awakening) I asked him why he was driving without a license since he knew better. He looked at me and said, "did you ever feel like you just had to get up and go - just go somewhere?" I thought to myself, go where?

I told him that I do not recall thinking that way too much, but if I did - and, knowing how the law views unlicensed drivers, I would not do it myself unless I had a valid license if I was the one driving. He proceeded to tell me that he did not think it was any big deal, since he was doing so good "out there" anyway. In fact, he stated that "I didn't hurt nobody, so what's the big deal?" The problem is, as with many violators - what the inmate many times considers "no big deal", obviously is a big deal to police and parole agents. And, to make matters worse, the attitudes of many inmates toward these "no big deal" issues and items seem to dominate their actions at times and override their good common sense and reasoning ability to what ever degree it exists.

It should be clarified at this point, that not all parole violators return due to intentional or irresponsibly induced violations. There are for example, men who leave on parole and remain in close association with other parolees or ex-offenders, who tend to treat them better than family members do in some cases, if they even have family members. This is a sad statement of society, but many times the case. The basic needs are being met by people who the law says the parolee is not to be in close contact with, nevertheless it is a violation - and can cause the parolee to be returned to jail.

On the other hand, there are those who are, or have been in the past, involved in various levels of drug use and sales. It should be understood that everyone does not sell drugs so they can live lavishly and drive expensive vehicles. In fact, a good number of those involved in drug trade do not live like that. The image portrayed by television of the palacial living standard with cars, jewelry, and an abundance of beautiful women is common to but a few out of all who are involved in drug trade. There are those who afford a few extra luxuries of life with it. There are those who feed their own drug habit with it - and everything in between. In fact at the present time, about half of all the people coming to jail on a new charge or returning on parole violations are connected somehow with drugs. By statistic, as of 1994, nearly 60% of all federal prisoners and 25% of all state prisoners were serving time for drug convictions. By comparison in 1980, drug convictions only accounted for approximately 5% of all state and federal jail populations. The abundance of drugs and the profits made from them are in many cases just too much for many to resist.

The main thing we must understand is that drug use and sales is as much economically induced as it is socially or psychologically. Whether the dollar is the sole purpose for one getting up in the morning or just to pay bills and get by, it is difficult to compete by means of legitimate profession or other legal enterprising venture with the rapid and abundant cash flow that drug sales offer. The only drawback is, there are various

173

complications and dangers associated with this high risk avenue of income.

I had an inmate tell me one time that he was then 24 years old, and had been dealing in drugs since he was 19. It was his first time in jail, and he seemed to sincerely hate it. He stated that he wanted to go back out and earn an honest living, and watch his children grow up to be better people than himself. He was looking into various professions and schooling to get into. He related to me that in the last year before coming to jail, he was clearing approximately $15 - $20,000 in cash per week after his supplier was paid. No college, no high school diploma, and no desire for such - until ending up in jail. "It's too late once you arrive here to turn back the clock", he said. "Now, there's no one to watch out for my wife and little kids, and I'm stuck here."

He stressed once again that he just wants to get out of jail and make an honest living, because it just isn't worth it having to come to jail. He told me the sad part about it is, that he only has about $9,000 and four small properties to show for all the money that passed through his hands through the years. He now realizes that he could have paid cash for an education at any school of his choice, and still be a free man enjoying the niceties of life rather than sitting in a jail cell for years to come.

He stressed one thing to me about the drug business that many people overlook or just do not realize. He said, "drugs are easy money. Probably the easiest and quickest money there is to be made in society today. You do not need an education or any credentials to be in business. You have no overhead, and as quick as you can make a delivery, you made money. You work whenever you want and name your own salary. People do not sell drugs because they are black, poor, illiterate, or dumb. They sell drugs because of the fast and easy money they bring. I had customers who were bank executives and customers who were street people. It makes no difference. It's all about addiction - to the drug, to money, or both."

At this point in the conversation, I realized how tough it is to try and convince someone who is used to this fast and easy money - and especially with no education or skills - that the honest way is the best way. Try to persuade someone with no education making hundreds or thousands of dollars a day in drugs, that a $5.00 per hour job at a fast food restaurant is a better way to go. It seems that many out in society today involved in drug activity would rather risk going to jail, or dying in some unfortunate way due to disease or murder, rather than choose the fast food restaurant or further education.

Unfortunately, this is one of the evils of the drug trade. Because it presents such an enticing and irresistible invitation to many people in society, whether they barely earn enough to live on or are very well off, it seems to entwine people of all races and financial status. To reverse someone's thinking or persuade and convince one who is involved in this fast money is in many or most cases a miracle and monumental task.

The use of drugs has of course become very prevalent throughout society, whether it be for stimulatory, euphoric, sedative, or health maintenance purposes. As life becomes more difficult to deal with for many, drugs provide an avenue of adaptability to all of the pressures and problems that accompany it. Unfortunately, many of these illegal drugs throughout the controlled substance realm are very dangerous, very costly, and addictive - contributing to a large number of crime and violations due to sales and use, and of course contributing to many more people coming to jail than ever before.

There are also those cases where a violation which sent a man back to prison at the hand of one parole officer, might have just been handled by a warning at the hand of another. It is the feeling of many inmates and staff, that bringing someone back to jail for a minor offense if they are working and assuming responsibility on the street is not justified - especially with prison overcrowding as it is presently. In some cases, this tends to discourage inmates when they are attempting to do better; especially when they feel that the parole agent is being overbearing or very unfair in their particular situation, and eventually they just give up and figure it's easier to do the time in jail rather than on the street.

Regardless of why the inmate was returned to prison, it does not negate the fact that a violation has most likely occurred, and the responsibility on the part of the inmate was not displayed to prevent their return. For the very few who are indeed innocent but had no strong alibi, dealing with incarceration must be doubly difficult. For those who are indeed guilty at levels to some degree, being on the inside looking out presents yet another challenge to life. The extra obstacle of incarceration has now been added to the already impending road blocks on the highway to happiness and contentment. Situations, that in some cases got out of control, or were already out of control due to early environmental problems encompassing various areas of negativity, eventually culminated into the now regretful and sorrowful situation of serving jail time.

These examples and facsimiles thereof bring us back to the same basic but overwhelming, complex concept - rehabilitation. Unlike rehabilitating someone from an unfortunate accident, where the main focus is getting bones to heal and tissues to mend and function again, we are talking here about actually changing the way a person thinks - which in turn has an effect on values, morals, standards, and their very actions in society. Once you are able to change their actions into a positive direction, you can then alter the effect they have on all nature. They will then begin to treat humans and animals with respect, and not just treat humans like animals with no respect. They will consider the fact that if they want to be treated with respect, they too must respect others. They will begin to understand that if they constantly judge themselves and their own actions, they will not have to be judged by others. With a change of attitude secondary to a change of heart and mind, they could easily be a free person many times instead of an incarcerated one.

The inmates that I have gotten to know over the years come from very diverse backgrounds. A wide variety of all types of people live in jail, but all have just one thing in common. They all were convicted of a crime or crimes, and sentenced to do time as a punishment. That is where the challenge begins. The challenge on the part of the inmate to decide to change the course of his or her life, and use this jail time to their advantage in preparing to live right from now on. Also, the challenge on the part of the corrections system to make available all the

176

possible tools needed to offer inmates a new start in life. Everyone needs a second chance, but unfortunately it takes the route of incarceration for some to realize they blew it the first time - or in some cases the second, third, or fourth time. There will always be circumstances beyond our immediate control that will be adversely effected by environment, standards, morals, and principles that we live by, but we nevertheless need a second chance to correct our error and begin to take our rightful place in society. Certain crimes, if one is convicted, do indeed carry long or severe penalties by law, but that does not say that change is not still needed. Whether it be physical, mental, or emotional, during freedom or incarceration, we need to constantly have a changing and renewing of our minds and hearts to walk the path of accountability and responsibility, so as to avoid the road that leads to penitentiary living. As a penalty for rebellion and disobedience, or conditions of sin as some refer to them, some people end up going the route of jail due to bad decisions they made and the actions that followed. It is only later that some discover that their way was not the accepted way, and they must change their thinking on certain issues if they do not desire making jail their permanent home.

As strange as it may sound, I've had a few inmates actually tell me that due to their lifestyles, it was very fortunate for them that they were arrested and sent to jail. They said if that had not happened, they would probably be dead. They confessed that jail has caused them to sit back and examine their "filthy", "wicked" lives (as one inmate put it) and have come to see the drastic need to change. That of course, is the first step in rehabilitation. A recognition of wrong or guilt must occur running paralleled with revelation for the need to change. You must admit you are wrong or see the need to change, or else, why change? Why would you change anything if you are happy or content with it?

Unfortunately, many inmates view their lives and habits in just that way. They see no need to change, and jail for many seems to be a temporary setback or restraint to life as they know it, but if they are not serving long sentences, they seem many times to return to the street and continue the same lifestyle that contributed to their incarceration in the first place. Some do not see the need or advantage in trying to change, due to the fact that they feel they made it this far and they will bounce back again somehow. They have not gotten the revelation through confinement, that if they do not change their habits and lifestyles, time periods of physical freedom could become less and less.

So, what role is corrections playing in offering inmates something that they can go home with, and lead productive lives in a lawful way? In reality, not much. Jail usually does not provide much in the way of correction, but rather lends to degrees of corruption by the very nature of its environment.

The title of "Corrections" tends to give a mere glimpse of hope to what we would like to see happen, rather than in reality what really does happen. Remember - jail does not breed honest, upright people - just as a bar room does not breed straight thinking, sober people. The quality of life in jail is equivalent to-the quality of life in jail. The quality going in is the quality going out at best. The input will determine the output - unless the quality of the input is altered before leaving. All too many times in the system as it is now, with the rehabilitative effort appearing to be at a minimum or even non-existent, the quality of the product leaving is even less than when it entered. Don't forget - jail is also like a big school. There are many things to learn with all the time people have, and whether you embrace positive or negative input is up to you. Unfortunately, the negative input that exists usually outweighs the positive, and each individual must make the decision as to what they feed their minds with. To paraphrase a statement made once by convicted and executed killer Ted Bundy - "Whatever you tend to feed your mind with and dwell on, is eventually what you will become."

In most jail settings, the potential for positive input is very limited. When you lock up hundreds and thousands of individuals together, all with various degrees of criminal history activity, you can imagine what general conversation has to offer. General conversation most common to the jail setting when its not about sports - usually embraces "sex, drugs, and rock and roll", in all forms and fashions, with a bland but steady diet of criminal activity talk mixed in. You can bet that whatever you do not know about illegal activity when entering the jail environment, you can seek out and learn while incarcerated, as many do. Many who come to jail, especially from the inner city, are already street smart, and the jail environment provides the opportunity to refine and educate them even more to the ways of the street and various types of activity not conducive to the laws of society. Consequently, many tend to leave the jail environment with good intentions, but are as bad or worse than when they arrived. If they have not stimulated their minds with positive input and educated themselves with scholastically based material or a trade, their chances of returning to prison are far greater. Unfortunately the system falls far short of being able to provide the needed resources and input for an attempt at large scale mental and psychological rehabilitation.

As previously mentioned, prisons are not rehabilitation facilities. They emphasize working and exercising as a means of passing time and relieving stress. Prisons are a bountiful source of physical rehabilitation when combining the exercise and sports options with the time to utilize them. As most of us realize, the emphasis on sports and recreation in this country is so great, that little time remains in many peoples lives for reading, studying, and improving the mind on a scholastic and intellectual level. If you can throw a football, hit a baseball or shoot hoops, you're in. Who cares if you can write your name or add and subtract, as long as you can play sports? This ideal is beginning to take a stronghold even in the pre-school ages now, and only gets worse through the years. Unfortunately, television helps to promote this and other disillusioning and distracting input which is influencing people in the wrong direction; as evidenced by some of the deviate lifestyles we see and hear about today, and some of the bizarre crimes that are being committed throughout society.

In prison of course, we have many excellent athletes. Some of the best boxers, football and basketball players, and weight lifters are living in jails across the country. In fact, our state institutions throughout Pennsylvania offer many structured athletic programs and organized sports, including football, baseball, basketball, softball, volleyball, track, wresting, boxing, and weight lifting. The free time that inmates have and the opportunity, both present themselves to these incarcerated people to reach their full potential physically and athletically. But what about mentally and psychologically?

Yes - mental rehabilitation - now that's the big challenge. Instead of building a man's back and biceps, we should be striving to build his brain power and intellect - if you want to present to him something to give him at least a fighting chance to stay out of jail and change his or her life for the better. Remember, if you want to change a persons character and actions, you must change the way they think and feel, and not just the way they look or perform physically.

In my opinion, which is shared by many others also, things such as sports and cable television should be for the most part earned privileges, which would follow confirmed literacy and the ability to communicate. When a man who just arrived in prison and can barely speak or write his name, has one thing on his mind, and that is "how do I get to the weight pile? ", something is drastically wrong. The last thing this man needs is a pile of weights, but rather a moderate pile of books and homework, so he can leave jail with more than muscle. Or, in another vivid example, a new arrival desperately needed to get his hands on a television so he could keep in touch with his M.T.V. and favorite crime show programs. After doing a little research and finding out that he was here for armed robbery and other related offenses, I quickly concluded that the last thing on earth this guy needed was a TV. to feed his mind more criminal strategy, fueled by the degenerate sub-culture lyrics of some of the music video's that are regularly shown.

Or, take for example, the fellow who regularly orders as many porn-related magazines as the system allows him, which again should not be permitted, so he can continue to fuel his already sex-crazed thoughts and desires and take his imagination to the max. The fact that some of these subscribers are already doing time for sex related crimes, with some including homicide and/ or children, does not seem to ring a bell with the system that this is definitely a detriment, and is as non-rehabilitative as you can get. I can recall the time I had to go to the Mental Health Unit, which houses individuals who cannot be placed in general population due to their mental health status, and/or types of crimes they committed in some cases. I happened to glance up at the television in the day room, and as a handful of these mental health patients watched intently, the guy on the T.V. proceeded to hack off a few heads and limbs of innocent people and proceeded to bury the evidence. As I watched the faces of these mentally disturbed patients actually reflect excitement and pleasure during that scene, I totally failed to recognize any rehabilitative qualities or positive re-enforcement in what they were watching. Should we really wonder why these people return again with crimes as bad or worse than before?

The last thing you want to do if you have any thought of rehabilitation is to re-enforce the very things that brought the people to prison in the first place. The ideas that television, drugs, and pornography help to pacify the overcrowded masses since it is so much a part of the culture anyway, is totally absurd. If the system even hopes to begin to rehabilitate anyone, it desperately needs to start rectifying and not just pacifying. Correctional systems across America need to recognize and respond to the actual needs, and not just the preferred ones. At the present time, we prefer to just lock the convicted criminal up as a punishment, and hope that he or she changes their minds about crime. As we readily see, that just isn't working.

Comparatively speaking, it's like throwing a loud, barking dog who keeps the neighborhood up at night into a kennel with other loud, barking dogs, and hoping that if he stays there long enough, he will think twice about barking all night and waking up the neighbors. You might say "well, that comes naturally to the animal, he's been doing it all his life." But, so it is also with some criminals. They have been exposed to and involved in criminal activity for so long, it now is second nature. It is now easier to do wrong than to do right, and thus the cycle of illegal activity perpetuates itself. It might have started out at a very young age with lying, cheating, or a little theft here and there, but eventually led to bigger things. The sex offender who was convicted of raping and killing the victim, did not just decide one day to go commit a rape/homicide. That crime was in the making long before it ever happened, fueled by a history of reading porn material, watching sex of all degrees on film, personal experimentation, and a constant mental ingestion of sexual thoughts and fantasies.

As proven over and over again, just locking the individual up for a period of time, and worst of all still giving them access to mental and physical stimulation for continued fantasy and negative input, will not change their way of thinking along those lines. In other words, the element of time, many and most times, does not cure the ill. A reprogramming - new insertion of thoughts, ideas, morals, ideals, and goals must be occurring to actually rehabilitate the person from their old nature and ways.

The young gang member at 16 or 17 years of age who is now doing big time for killing a rival gang member, did not just get up one morning and decide to waste a guy, to put it bluntly. With the help of a sub-standard living environment, all conditions considered, this individual, like thousands of others, began his criminal career much prior to the day of the homicide. It may have started with being exposed to guns and weapons at an early age, and learning of their use in illegal and unacceptable ways. The knowledge of the destructive force and sometimes false security that they can offer, can and did in many cases lead up to a senseless murder and now life in prison for the perpetrator.

Television and movies in some cases may have fueled the good guy gets bad guy fantasies, and the quest for justice became ever present. At some point, when rage, anger, fear, frustration, and whatever other emotions involved took precedence over common sense and self-control, the shooting occurred in an instant. Maybe with malice, maybe without, but nevertheless a body has to be answered for. A lifetime of incarceration can never wipe away all the emotions and feelings both leading up to the crime and remaining after the fact, unless the void is filled with other positive input. Just locking the perpetuator up and keeping them out of society is not going to negate what happened, or guarantee that it will not happen again in another circumstance. It merely serves as punishment for the crime.

We tend to think in this society that by making prisons tougher, harder places to live, and removing and restricting inmate privileges, that we are getting tough on crime and criminals. People place in high esteem, the Governors and law makers that desire to make inmates suffer for their wrongs. Granted, prison should not be a walk in the park. Prison life should be conducive to making the inmate feel the effect of crime by way of punishment through confinement and restricted privileges. But let us not forget that prison is after the fact, or post-crime penitence so to say. Ideally, the only real effective way to curb crime is for society to work to prevent the criminal act in the first place - to come between the perpetrator and the crime. People must be taught and educated to respect the humanity of others, and handle their disputes without violence. For this to take place, just as in rehabilitation in the post crime status, a new way of thinking is needed. A new respect for God and humanity must take place.

Rehabilitation for an individual is as individual as the individual themselves. Rehabilitation in most, if not all cases, does not just pertain to correcting some bad habits he or she picked up some time back. In many cases, habits and characteristics that lead to substance abuse, alcohol abuse, and/or criminal activity usually generate from seeds planted in early childhood. People tend to disregard or frown at statements like "I don't know why I did it", or "I couldn't help it", or even "I didn't mean to do it - it just happened." In reality, some of these statements are the actual truth. Due to some of the bad seeds planted in early childhood by parents, relatives, teachers, friends, and of course the television media, and fueled in some cases by drug and alcohol abuse-the bad end result has now surfaced. The growth of those bad seeds planted years ago is now producing a harvest-and in many cases, a bad one. The lack of guidance, discipline, and education, along with the lack or even absence of love, morals, and God conscious teaching, is producing an angry generation of young people unlike any before them. We see the evidence of this when reading about 6 year old children stabbing other children over a doll, or a 10 or 12 year old shooting another

183

child because they "dissed" them, or disrespected them as it stands for. This is the next generation that is going to be filling up the prison systems nationwide. This is a scary thought, even to other inmates.

In short, these are the kinds of people headed for the prison system in the near future. These are the humans that prison officials and other inmates are going to have to deal with, no matter how inhumane they may seem. We need rehabilitation. Things cannot and will not get any better without it. As time moves on, even the older inmates, who have helped to maintain order within the jails and have steered some of the younger convicts in the right direction, are not going to be around any more, due to release or death, which will leave the younger, angrier generation as the majority in the prison population.

So, exactly what is available to inmates at the present time in the way of programs or avenues of learning, educational improvement, and positive re-enforcement as a rehabilitative effort?

According to a published statistical report in 1995, the D.O.C. does place emphasis on inmates acquiring a basic education before being released. Unfortunately, it is not mandatory, and many do not take advantage of the free time they have to learn to read and write. Also, and again unfortunately, we see staffing needs at Graterford and possibly other institutions as well, that are not being met to make education available to all who wish to acquire it. I know of situations where inmates have been turned away from the school due to full classes and not enough teachers. This tends to discourage inmates who are seeking to do better, and certainly does not contribute to self improvement.

The report also makes note of a program throughout the system known as the Laubach Literacy Concept of "each one-teach one", which incorporates inmate tutors to teach others how to read. It is a known fact that for years even before any programs were introduced to the system, that inmates were the sole teachers in many cases, teaching others in the population to read, write, and do math. I know of cases even on death row years ago, where totally isolated men taught each other to read

184

and write by verbal communication, and at times letters or numbers carved in a bar of soap or a message taped to a bar of soap and slid from cell to cell on the floor, serving as the black board for visual learning. As primitive as this method may sound, one of these men I'm speaking of came to jail illiterate, and upon his eventual commutation and release, went on to earn a master's degree from a university.

The report also mentions a "Time to Read" program sponsored by Time - Life Inc., an innovative basic reading skills program, and being successful as a pilot program at SCI-Camp Hill, it was expanded to SCI-Muncy.

These programs and others like them are certainly needed throughout all the jails, but unfortunately appear to lack the personal funding and overall use that is needed to attempt to educate the thousands throughout the system who badly need it. It appears to be a good start, but there is certainly a long way to go.

According to the report, 16 of the institutions are presently offering post secondary studies, most of which are an associate degree program. One of the institutions offers a bachelor's degree program, and a couple of others offer a specialization certificate in areas such as plumbing, heating and air conditioning, electricity, and building or business management. Twenty - two out of the twenty three institutions offer various vocational training in a wide variety of fields, but again there are limitations. Inmates are frequently turned down for apprenticeship programs due to not possessing a G.E.D. or high school diploma. Programs many times are full, thus creating a waiting list. According to qualifications, the inmate must also have at least 18 months left to serve in the institution before release or parole, or they will not be accepted. There is also a 90 day probationary period with an apprenticeship program, basically to evaluate the inmates work habits and character, and even though he or she may pass the probationary period, a dismissal is possible at anytime during the apprenticeship period if certain regulations are not followed.

The system also offers assistance and counseling to inmates by way of sex offender and specialized sex offender programs and treatment. According to the report, drug and alcohol programs exist throughout the entire system, serving some 9,500 inmates at various levels of treatment.

At SCI-Graterford, we have what is known as the Jericho program, geared toward people with drug and alcohol addictions and various character disorders. It is basically a 12 to 18 month program depending on the progress of each individual and operates with very stringent rules. Being a therapeutic commit, (T.C.), the inmates are housed in a separate area from the general population. They have their own exercise yard, and have very little contact with anyone outside those in the program. Other than for a visit to the chapel, medical needs, or an outside visit by family or friends, the inmates remain in the unit. There are never more than 50 inmates enrolled in the program at one time, making it easier to police their actions and give more individual attention to inmates if and when the need arises.

By statistic, roughly a 75% success rate has been demonstrated when checking the progress of those who completed the program and were evaluated one year later. For the sake of comparison, there are programs outside the jail system that are only claiming a 25-30 percent success rate at best, and of course, some are less. One that I have known of, and had friends who actually went through, is the program called Teen Challenge. Detailed in a book entitled "The Jesus Factor", written by its founder David Wilkerson, this program claims success rates of 80 - 90 percent, even after individuals have been out seven years. This program known and established nationwide, was even studied by the U.S. Government due to its amazing success rates.

These are the types of programs with such success rates, that are needed on a much larger scale throughout the prison systems, so that incarcerated individuals can begin seeing an existence and purpose beyond drugs, alcohol, and various behavior disorders that contributed to them coming to jail in the first place. The report also makes mention of in-house forensic mental health units at a few of the institutions, with a variety of support services involving mental health care throughout the entire system. Also, primarily geared to Vietnam War Veterans, a Post

Traumatic Stress Disorder program (PTSD) is in force. In fact, Graterford now has the only PTSD treatment group in the entire state prison system, since it was discontinued at two of the other institutions that were involved along with Graterford previously.

All of these programs and opportunities are surely a good start, and a good attempt at meeting all the diverse needs of the thousands of inmates throughout the system. Unfortunately, it appears as if it is only the tip of the iceberg. Society in general is becoming more intimidated by crime and criminals, and is desperately seeking a solution to the ever growing problem of recidivism and prison overcrowding.

Some feel it is definitely time in the world we live in today and within the corrections system, to take a strong look at some serious steps in rehabilitation. Crime is not decreasing and prisons are not getting smaller or less in number. It is not so important that we build good bodies beyond reasonable physical exercise, but rather build strong minds and good character. Minds and hearts that turn away from crime and criminal activity, and not run toward it.

To achieve such results, we must look at ways to create more vocational and technical training programs within institutions if we expect to give inmates anything at all to go back out with and make a living rather than making their living from crime. Basic primary and secondary education should be an entry level standard, so that inmates do not leave, or stay, which ever the case may be, and remain as illiterate as when they arrived. Varying opinions exist on whether higher education (post high school studies) should be readily available to just any inmate who desires to learn for the sake of learning, some due to having excessive time on their hands. Undergraduate and post graduate studies could prove very useful in some cases, and might even be useful in a merit system where sentence time could be shortened upon achieving certain degree levels. Taking into consideration that prisons are overcrowded, preparation for certain occupations could possibly help to put some people back into society as productive, tax paying citizens prior to serving their entire sentence. Undoubtedly, strict guidelines would have to be set up as to qualifications and feasibility of future use, due to the expense incurred with course work. In my opinion, any inmate who would choose to pay for courses themselves, should have the privilege of taking them just as civilians do. In other words, higher education is good, but not always at the expense of the taxpayers. The end result must equally be examined and evaluated to determine and set priorities and guidelines.

Creating incentives among inmates will always result in a positive move toward rehabilitation. Whether is creates incentive to get off drugs, get an education, or merely get a job, it is creating incentive. Of course, as far as income is concerned, jobs must be available to attain in the first place if an inmate is attempting to live by the law. Government and economics are a whole different issue not to be discussed at this time. Nonetheless, any program that can give inmates any kind of positive input and outlook could only prove to be an asset. When we begin to restrict and remove privileges that have been earned through time, merit, and self-discipline, desire and incentive likewise tend to decrease. Inmates are like any other human beings, in that they thrive on and become productive on reward and purpose, not just punishment. One thing inmates do not need, especially considering the way some of them grew up, is one more blow to their fragile egos, or something they view as one more setback in life's constant fight for survival and a sense of purpose.

Prison mental health experts that I have talked to personally, including psychiatrists, psychologists, and counselors, all seem to agree that many of the system's inmates could be rehabilitated if the proper resources were available to work with. Unfortunately, much of this resource availability is based on economics, and we all know what part economics plays in most areas of society today.

There are inmates in jails anywhere who are many times labeled "hopeless cases", and viewed as unrehabilitative due to low I.Q., aberrant personalities, and previous life styles that display constant criminal tendencies and criminal activity. When examining the many inmates that have had chance after chance and still cannot conform to societies guidelines, it appears as if continual punishment is the only other option.

When judging by the clinical histories of these individuals, keeping them locked up seems like the only way. Basically, non-conformists by record, who certainly do not seem interested in changing for the better and living by the prescribed law.

Since many or most inmates tend to display sociopathic behavior to varying degrees, the challenge and task of rehabilitation on a large scale again becomes monumentally harder due to the individual attention needed for each inmate. Rehabilitation within the present system certainly does not occur by system design, but rather personal choice and individual desire to change. There are those few who make the decision to change whatever they need to in their lives and their thinking to keep jail from being their home address, but it is indeed few out of all who are locked up.

Could these statistics change with more and better resources available? Experts feel sure that they could. Would tax paying society benefit by an expensive, aggressive, extensive and comprehensive re-organization of the present system, if geared primarily on rehabilitating instead of just incarcerating? Only time would reveal such statistics. Experts feel that is impossible to predict, since it has never been attempted on any sizeable scale. With the DOC's budget rapidly approaching one billion dollars in the next two or three years, the idea of introducing and funding more and more programs on a large scale for any reason is hard to imagine.

In a report issued by the Pennsylvania Commission on Corrections Planning (PCCP) in December of 1993, the conclusion was made that there are only two paths to follow:

1. "build at least five more prisons at a twenty year cost of $4 billion, (which was in addition to the seven additional ones already scheduled to be operating by 1995);
2. develop and fund new alternatives that promote hard work, discipline, and education and discourage idleness, hopelessness, and substance abuse."

For comparison's sake, in 1971 the DOC employed 2,268 people. By the year 2000, the roster is projected to approach approximately 12,000. As of 1993, the state of Pennsylvania was spending approximately $6,127 per year to educate one child. As of 1995, it was spending approximately $22,900.00 to keep one inmate for one year.

Either we spend millions of dollars to punish criminals and make an all out attempt to release people back into society who will become productive, contributing individuals, or we spend millions of dollars just to punish criminals - period. Either way, society will pay-it is just a question of how to spend the money and what you hope to accomplish.

We do not need any more weight lifters, but rather something or someone to begin lifting the weight - off individuals, off the correctional system, and off society as a whole. It is the opinion of many that we as a society must begin looking at other alternatives, since the system as it exists now is just not working; as evidenced by each human life it takes in and holds captive to large scale abundant negative input. We must never forget that many of the people who populate jails today will be returning to society someday. The system has the opportunity to cultivate and play a big part in the kind of individuals these people will re-enter society as - whether it be positive and productive, or negative and counter productive.

That again is where rehabilitation comes in. It has been proven over and over again, that if you can redirect a persons thinking and ideals into a positive flow, their physical being will follow along. You then begin to see them give more serious thought to important things in life such as education, the family unit, a serious devotion to God the Creator, and the need and desire to assume responsibility as they should. This would then begin to reflect less people committing crimes, and more people remaining on the street as parolees due to assuming the responsibility they need to in everyday life, especially until they are off parole status.

Imagine the relief the justice system would feel, particularly in the realm of corrections facilities, if it were locking up fewer people for new crimes and many of the ones that are leaving never returned. It is a fact that we will always need jails, due to some people's rebellious attitudes toward change, and people will continue to be removed from society due to illegal actions. For some, this change in address so to say, is not only necessary for penitence and repentance, but for their very survival due to their hardness of heart. No matter what the environment, some people are not environmentally safe, nor user friendly.

Maybe it is time to at least make an attempt at restoring life within the ranks of the incarcerated, so that life beyond the prison confines does not seem so impossible, and criminal activity does not appear as an alternative, much less the only alternative.

The Realm of Conviction

As the Judge imposes the sentence deemed appropriate by law, the man found guilty appears lifeless as he stares straight ahead in a moment of disbelief. What seems like a review of his entire life story now just flashed through his mind in a matter of seconds. What sounded like a few sniffles accompanying a common cold just seconds earlier, now has evolved into a chorus of blatant crying and sobbing throughout the courtroom. Whatever distant hope he might have had of escaping the demise of serving time, has just seemingly vanished into thin air.

Charged, tried, convicted, sentenced, and now ready to begin serving the penalty imposed for the conviction.

This individual, like many thousands of others yearly, has entered the realm of conviction known as prison. His life will now change from a state of freedom to a state of confinement. His thoughts and decisions will no longer encompass things like what kind of car to buy or where to go on vacation, but rather things like what snacks or cosmetics to buy in the prison commissary, or how to maintain or assist his loved ones now that he is incarcerated, or possibly just trying to find peace and retain sanity in such an unpeaceful, depressed environment.

This "realm of conviction" that most people never experience in a lifetime, is a combination of chaos, turmoil, loneliness, frustration, despair, anxiety, stress, and depression, all rolled up into one agonizing package. Locking hundreds and thousands of individuals up in a closed neighborhood such as prison against their will could produce little more than that. In this realm, hundreds and thousands of people with every like and dislike, trust and distrust, attitude, prejudice, and bad intention, must cohabitate and find some level of existence and self-worth where many times there seems to be none at all. The odds are that anyone who lives in the prison environment for any length of time and survives such a test will definitely leave - if and when they leave - a different person. Even if incarcerated for life, the person now on the more elderly and of the scale will be a much different one from the one who entered.

What is it about prison that causes this metamorphosis of personality and attitude? Some say the restrictions. Some say the separation from family, friends, and the outside world in general. Others attribute it to the insanity of jail life as a whole.

I heard a man say one time that the worst part of jail for him was having to come out of his cell. He said he gets tired of being careful of how he looks at someone, or what he says to someone, or even how he walks by certain people, being cautious not to give an impression of weakness, or having an attitude. He said "attitudes" here will get you in big trouble, especially if you can't back them up."

Likewise, I had a man tell me one time that the worst part for him was having to go into his cell. He said one of his greatest fears in jail was being locked in his cell during a fire or emergency situation, and being at the mercy of the staff for his survival.

I had yet another tell me once that his worst nightmare was being separated from his wife and children. He said as vulnerable as he felt coming to the prison environment, he knew that his family was even more at risk in the "big city". He said that doing what he did to come to jail was bad enough, but the separation and limited contact with his family was far worse.

This is a common fear shared by many who become incarcerated. The loss of friends and loved ones is an all too often occurrence for those who come to jail. I can't begin to count the men who told me through the years that they have experienced this temporary or permanent separation, due to incarceration.

The prison environment as it exists today seems at times to be more detrimental to one's well being than it is instrumental in creating better people of the ones who have entered. With the rehabilitation effort at a minimum, many inmates' minds are hanging in a stagnant state rather than being stimulated creatively. Life can get pretty boring when all you do is get up, eat, possibly exercise, and in some cases, do some sort of menial work for a few cents per hour. This does not exactly occupy one's mind to the fullest and prepare them to re-enter society a better person, or a productive one either. For the most part, the prison environment tends to be a breeding ground for more of the same thinking and rationale that it already incarcerates. Lawmakers, law enforcers, and free society in general tend to believe that if they just get the "bad people" off the street, that the world will be a better place to live. What they tend to overlook is that most of these "bad people" who are in jail will eventually go back to the street; and chances are with rehabilitation at a minimum, they will return to society as yet potentially more "bad people". Prison in many cases does not change the "bad people", but just alters their course a little. I think we have seen by now that warehousing convicted criminals and not challenging their minds in a positive, constructive way is basically a fruitless attempt at dealing with crime and its effects. Compared to a bandaid on cancer, it just does not stop the disease from spreading.

The other amazing thing about these "bad people" in jails - as some label them - is that everyday, we are receiving more and more "bad people" from society. With new commits and parole violators, the line waiting to come in has no end. This makes a strong statement as to the fact that all of the "bad people" are not in jail yet. No matter how many we continue to sentence and lock up, there are still more waiting to come in. In reality, and as much as people hate to face the fact, society is loaded with people just like the ones that are locked up in jails anywhere. After all, where did they all come from in the first place?

All around us, everywhere we travel and cohabitate, are people who have been engaged in criminal activity in the past, or are presently, engaged in various criminal activity, but just never stepped over that fine line that separates freedom from incarceration. Some have committed heinous acts and have escaped getting caught. Others, fully understanding the consequences to be had, continue to play their hand to illicit and criminal activity until the law decides they have played enough. There are many hostile, angry, abused people moving about in society today just looking for a vent for their frustrations. Unfortunately, depending on how they choose to vent their frustrations, " the realm of conviction " called jail may not be far away.

Remember, anyone has the potential and ability to commit a criminal act. Some spontaneous, some accidental, others pre-meditated, but nevertheless, the potential and ability do exist. Whether these penalty-worthy or jail-worthy acts ever actually occur or not, is for the most part regulated by each individuals "personal convictions". Strong convictions against dishonesty and any type of criminal activity can many times help one to avoid what some label the "ultimate conviction" - being found guilty and sent to prison. A realm of conviction that has been all too real for some, and even more than once in many cases.

An inmate told me once that incarceration makes you take a second look - at yourself, at your actions, at your situation, and at life in general. He told me that jail has made him evaluate and establish priorities. This particular inmate, like thousands of others, has many years to serve before even thinking about any kind of freedom, and has no choice but to do the time. "What you make of it means everything", he said. "It has made me realize that there are laws and standards that must be followed; and because I didn't follow them, now I'm here. I made bad decisions and my conviction is the end result." Other than conviction as a result of bad actions, as in having to serve time, our normal "convictions" tend to serve as a guide for our actions every day of our lives. As we deal with life on an everyday basis, our decisions and actions leave us feeling either content or at peace with ourselves, or they may leave us feeling "convicted", or uneasy about certain things. People who have been fortunate enough to have good morals, ethics, and standards instilled in them at an early age, seem to be quickly "convicted" when a passing thought of illegal, immoral, or unlawful activity passes through their mind or becomes a temptation.

Those who lack these positive attributes many times seem to be more prone to activity which is not accepted by society in general. A "conviction" of the heart and mind before a crime or bad occurrence is far better to have to deal with than the conviction that could occur after the act - namely, incarceration.

I can vividly remember, after narrowly escaping arrest for retail theft back in 9th grade, the "conviction" I had for some period of time after the incident. I had been with some friends on other occasions when they stole things, and due to peer pressure, I too attempted to meet the challenge. If I did not do it, I was out of the circle, so to say. The problem was, the store owner was getting wise to our little group, and seeing our faces more than once, was also getting ready to nab us. We narrowly escaped by two different exits, since he and his wife just could not stop nor hold all of us at once until the police arrived. After such a close call, especially at that young age, I was so thankful that I did not get caught, that not only did I not do it again, but the thought of it, or any theft, flashed a big red flag in front of my face. I see that as a very healthy "conviction", and one less way of possibly becoming a "convict".

I saw at a later time how peer pressure was dominating and winning out over my convictions that I had acquired at a very young age. We were always taught never to steal, nor do anything that we would not want done to us.

Conviction does not only center around the jury reaching a guilty verdict or the gavel falling against the magistrates bench. Nor does it only count as a "win" when the prosecution is able to persuade a jury to think and vote to their advantage - thus finding a party guilty of some or all charges. Conviction is more than all that. In fact, the stronger the conviction we have to do things the proper, moral, legal way, the less chance we have of becoming involved in situations that could cause us to become a convict.

A person anywhere, anytime, may have the idea or opportunity to participate in an act deemed illegal and/or punishable by law. They become involved in this certain act and in time are arrested, charged, tried, and convicted. Another person anywhere, anytime, has the same opportunity for involvement, but backs out and avoids the temptation of the situation due to their conscience or "convictions".

One ends up being convicted by law due to "lack of conviction", and thus becomes a convict. The other ends up remaining free to enjoy life due to a greater sense of values and moral conviction. I think we all know which is the more desirable, and certainly no less tolerable type of "conviction".

Nonetheless, the cycle continues throughout all humanity, every second on through every century. People entering the world as babies in a convict-free status, and some later becoming convicts by their very actions, reactions, bad decisions, and lack of convictions - to self, to others, to the laws of society, and to God. Lack of conviction and commitment to God and His laws, impacts our capability to follow the rules and principles set forth to govern our society for the best. Thus, this lack of conviction lends way to consistent bad decision making and bad choices.

Decision and choice - two elements based largely on our morals and personal convictions centering around the Creator and his principles - two elements that ultimately can mean the difference between poverty and wealth, sickness and health, life and death, and of course in most cases, freedom and incarceration.

Jail is not hard to get into, but is growing ever harder to get out of. Laws, law makers, and law enforcers are increasing the odds that jails will continue to flourish, and crime will continue to be dealt with by way of more punishment through incarceration. It is reported that attempts are always being made to improve the quality of life for those incarcerated, striving at the same time to constantly insure and improve the safety factor for both employees and inmates. Nevertheless, prison is not, nor will it ever be, an environment considered by most to be a desired dwelling place.

SCI-Graterford by itself has seen many changes within the last few years, not to mention all the other institutions statewide making revisions in policy, procedure, and personnel. Some of the policies, procedures, and statistics throughout this book, will undoubtably have changed since the time of writing. The entire corrections industry is evolving and preparing to try to meet the ever changing demands that it is facing as it heads into a new century.

In essence, policy, procedure, statistics, and staff will continue to change; but prison operations remain basically the same. Jail is still jail, confinement is still confinement, and no matter how many changes are made to improve and upgrade the realms and reality of incarceration, the living conditions that jail could offer at its' very best could never outweigh or equal the benefits of being free. In short, a continuous living hell for many, with no sure end in sight.

Remember - the decisions and choices that we make this day, can and surely will effect the rest of our lives. Thus continues the circle of conviction.

Addendum

The following noteworthy changes, improvements, occurrences and updates regarding policy, procedure and previously stated statistics concerning Graterford and the entire D.O.C. were submitted just prior to printing. These were written in addendum form so as not to cause re-typing, re-editing, or any changes in mechanical layout, but still give the reader the benefit of updated facts available on certain issues just prior to publication.

1997 /98

* Residential Substance Abuse Treatment Program (RSAT) started at Graterford and other institutions throughout the state.

1998

* All lifers and violent offenders brought in from the Outside Service Unit (OSU) at Graterford and all institutions statewide. No lifers or inmates with violent offenses on their records (i.e. assault, rape, etc.) live or work outside the main fences or walls of the institutions.

* The State Correctional Institution at Chester (SCI-Chester) opens and receives the first inmates on April 27, 1998. It is considered a speciality institution designed to deal with inmates having serious substance abuse problems. The next institution slated to open - tentatively in the year 2000 - is SCI- Pine Grove in Western Pennsylvania. It is being opened to house young adult offenders under 21 years old.

* On May 18, 1998, the co-pay policy for inmate medical care was put into effect statewide, requiring inmates to contribute a specified amount of money toward their medical care.

* Introduction of mounted patrols at Graterford and three other institutions in the state. (As of summer, 1999, SCI-Graterford has six horses being used in patrol details.)

* Security measures increased at Graterford by way of video cameras and monitors, more metal detectors, added security posts, and increased searches.

1999

* Impact of crime program started at Gratertord, and will also be in other institutions throughout the state prison system.

As of now, it is a 22 week program which offers no credits and no certificate, but does teach inmates how their crimes impact the lives of others in their families, friends, victims families, and society in general. Survivors of crime volunteer to come and talk to the inmates along with program information and discussion.

* SCI-Graterford farm closed in early summer.

* Execution of Gary Heidnik in July. This becomes the third execution performed in Pennsylvania since that of Elmo Smith in 1962.

* New uniforms issued to Corrections Officers statewide - black and grey combination replaces the blue and grey colors worn for many years. (Some were issued as early as 1998).

* On August 2nd, Norman Johnston (four life sentences) escapes from SCI-Huntingdon and manages to evade capture for nearly four weeks. Two weeks after his escape, two more inmates (one a lifer, and one serving 20-50 years for arson) managed to escape from SCI-Dallas. Governor Ridge ordered the immediate lockdown of the entire state prison system and a thorough check of all perimeters, security systems, and security procedures. Searches were also conducted throughout the jails for contraband. Johnston used a cutting tool to cut bars on his cell window, then squeezed out and cut through two fences to escape. He also fabricated a dummy and placed it in his bed, which allowed his escape to go unnoticed for two head counts. Sources said it was about ten hours since anyone had talked to him and realized he was missing.

All three escapees were caught by September, and as a result of the dummy in the bed and the time lapse which allowed the escapees to go unnoticed for so long, it is now standard policy to do standing counts so the officers counting can see the inmate move, and not just assume that the body in the bed is a real person. Exceptions to the rule are those inmates that are bedridden for any reason, in which case the officer needs to confirm somehow that they are indeed a living being. Also, in dormitory - style housing, inmates are allowed to sit on the bed rather than stand.

Whenever escapes occur, it always makes officials take a second look at security systems and procedures. They simply need to know how it happened, and how to try and prevent it from happening again. This keeps the need and desire for developing and installing new security systems and procedures fresh at all times.

* Inside sources state that in the planning stage at the moment for Graterford, and most probably other jails in the state as well, is a new security system designed to be mounted around the inside perimeter of the wall or fence, and uses monitors and electrical current to further prevent escapes. The system basically uses three wires, one of which is a motion detector, and when sensing an intruder, sends an electrical current through the second wire in that particular section. If for some reason this does not stop the inmate and he or she is able to proceed, the third wire can then be charged manually with the push of a button, while watching the whole event on video. A system such as this could eventually eliminate the need for guard towers, and further insure the security of institutions against escapes.

Acknowledgements

Many thanks to Mr. "E" for his valuable input and contribution of time, for whatever was needed to help this project be real.

Many thanks to any staff members that contributed valuable information in the form of facts, statistics, stories, and critique, to help make this as complete and accurate as possible.

Many thanks to the inmates that participated by way of questionnaire, helping to reveal their thoughts and feelings on the issues that so many people are curious about.

Many thanks also to any inmates who offered valuable input and finite detail in any informal manner, helping to reveal the real side of incarceration and the system that controls the whole process.

Many thanks to my typist, who suffered through my pseudo - legible handwriting, and helped the story come together on paper.

Many, Many thanks to my wonderful wife for her valuable input on sentence structure and composition - and for just being my wonderful wife and mother to our children.

Many thanks to all who purchase this book. I hope it proves to be enjoyable and informative reading, and totally serving the purpose for which it was written.

References

I Pennsylvania Rules of Court (State) – West Publishing Company Copyright 1995

II West's Pennsylvania Practice (Vol. 2) - Criminal Procedure Forms and Commentary by D. Rudovsky and L. Sosnov West Publishing Co. - Copyright 1991

III Title 37 Pa. Code - Sect. 61.1 through Sect. 77.1 Under pt. II - Board of Probation and Parole - Specific Ref. to Sect. 65.4" General Conditions of Special Probation and Parole." Copyright 1988 Comm. of PA

IV 30th Anniversary Commemorative History. Commonwealth of Pennsylvania - Bureau of Correction "The Bureau of Correction and its Institutions" printed at SCI- Huntingdon - April 1983

V Commonwealth of Pennsylvania Commission on Corrections Planning Final report - Dec. 1993

VI The Need for Parole Options for Life-Sentenced Prisoners. Prepared by the Pennsylvania Prison Society's Policy and Planning Committee July 6, 1993

VII Pennsylvania Dept. of Corrections 1995 Annual Statistical Report

VIII 1996 PA Bureau of Correction Educational Programs - Adult Correctional Institutions

IX Report on Execution Warrants Issued by Governor (under 1978 capital punishment statute) period beginning Aug. 1 1985 thru Jan. 1,1996 (including Governors' Thomburgh, Casey, Acting Gov. Singel, and Governor Ridge at present.

X Pittsburgh Post – Gazette January 30, 1997 (Thursday) Edition Report concerning SCI-Pittsburgh Security Conditions and recent escape

XI Jewish Exponent April 21, 1995 Edition (Vol. 197, No. 16 / Phila., PA) Article entitled "Debating the Death Penalty"

About the Author

When beginning my career in Radiology in 1974 at the former Sacred Heart Hospital in Norristown, Pa., I never imagined that some day I would be working and supervising inmates in Pennsylvania's largest state correctional institution at Graterford (S.C.I.G) Hospitals, clinics, and offices surely presented many unique, exciting, educational, and unforgettable experiences over the 26 years, but none so unique as those " in prison."

In this diverse strata of society locked away from society, I began as a part-time contract employee of the state in 1981. I was the first civilian ever hired at SCI-G to perform the X-ray services, which were performed solely by inmates up until that time. Supervising and working closely with inmates from the very beginning provided me with "prisoner perspective" on prison life long before any civilian orientation ever occurred. Contract employees did not go to the training academy or have any orientation at that time, so much of what I learned about the "the system" and the way things really are in jail I learned from inmates first. Then as time went on, I learned how things are "supposed" to operate according to policy. The two tend to differ at times. In fact, I was given an employee handbook the first day I started and was told to learn it. That was my orientation.

Things have changed a lot since then and some of my views of life, and prison life in particular have greatly changed from those I held previously.

All "television" prison is not all real prison, though it does reveal some truths and occurrences sweetened with sensationalism to attract the viewer.

Realizing how uninformed I was with many distorted views on the whole subject before I began working in a jail, my whole intention in writing this book was to present the real side of prison. A true and factual unbiased presentation of prison, inmates, and the system and people that keep it going.

Hopefully, these facts, statistics, stories and real life experiences have accomplished just that.

"Very true and very accurate."
- Lifer with 26 years served

"Gives a very accurate picture of the operations and environment."
- 28 year staff member

"True and on – time."
- Lifer with 16 years served

"Exciting reading, good detail, and so true."
- 14 year staff member

"Gives a much better and truer picture of jail than the T.V. shows reveal."
- Inmate serving 20 to 40 year sentence

"It made me think twice about where I work."
- Staff member